Alexander Thomas Ormond

Basal Concepts in Philosophy

An Inquiry into Being, Non-Being, and Becoming

Alexander Thomas Ormond

Basal Concepts in Philosophy
An Inquiry into Being, Non-Being, and Becoming

ISBN/EAN: 9783337069131

Printed in Europe, USA, Canada, Australia, Japan

Cover: Foto ©Thomas Meinert / pixelio.de

More available books at **www.hansebooks.com**

BASAL CONCEPTS IN
PHILOSOPHY

BASAL CONCEPTS IN PHILOSOPHY

AN INQUIRY INTO BEING, NON-BEING, AND BECOMING

BY

ALEXANDER T. ORMOND, Ph.D.
PROFESSOR OF PHILOSOPHY IN PRINCETON UNIVERSITY

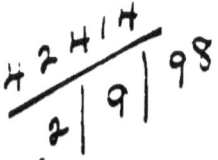

NEW YORK
CHARLES SCRIBNER'S SONS
1894

PREFACE

The motive of this volume is a desire to restore the primacy of certain conceptions which are in danger of disappearing from our modern thinking, and to reform others which, as I think, have been wrongly or inadequately conceived. Reflection has led me to dissent from monistic pantheism on the one hand, and from agnosticism on the other, two of the leading tendencies in the thought of our century, and to seek a metaphysical basis for philosophy that may adequately ground a rational theory of knowledge and being. With this end in view, I have sought to reconstruct philosophy upon the trinal categories of being, non-being, and becoming, and also to reform the current methods of metaphysics by showing that a completely rational idea of being can be achieved only when we represent it under our highest and most concrete categories and translate it into self-conscious personal spirit. The result is a spiritualistic metaphysic which leads us to ground the world of reality in an Absolute possessed of supreme intelligence, goodness, and love.

The order in which the basal concepts emerged in my own thinking, is substantially as follows: Having, by historic study and reflection, become convinced of the identity of the logos with the principle of conscious personality, I began to see its value as a means of penetrating the opaque absolute of the agnostic creed, and obtaining an intelligible conception of its inner nature and connection with the relative. The application of the logos-category led directly to the personal construction of being and to the idea of the Absolute as personal, self-conscious spirit. It was at this point that the dualistic light came to me in an intuition of the immanent movement or dialectic of spirit. For it became clear that the activity of a self-conscious spirit must be first of all intellectual, and that its primal intellection would be dual in its nature, including a positive intuition of being's self or the logos, and a negative intuition of its not-self or the a-logos. And reflection made it clear also that the logos and a-logos are primal and mutually exclusive opposites, and that while spiritual being is to be conceived as exercising internally the activity which intuites the positive and negative terms, yet the object of the negative intuition, the a-logos, must be excluded from being as its opposite; that is, as non-being.

The exclusion of non-being from being as its opposite, never to be identified with it, laid the foundations of a dualistic creed, and through it of a reform of spiritual dialectic in the direction of a non-pantheistic theory of creation and the connection of the Absolute with the sphere of relativity. For it became clear that the primal intuition of non-being would motive an outgo of volitional energy into the negative sphere for its suppression and annulment and that the nature generated out of it would not be pure being but becoming, a creature including in its constitution opposite moments of being and non-being. Thus, through the conception of the negative datum, I began to see that an answer might be forthcoming to the hitherto unresolved problem, why the creative energy of the Absolute falls short of an absolute result and only produces the finite and imperfect. The book itself must answer the question how far the solution is to be regarded as satisfactory. For the last, but not least important, insight I have to thank the great master of thinking, Aristotle. The identification of his category of self-activity with the nature of absolute and self-existent being, was the "holding turn" that reduced all the elements to final unity and coherence.

In the unfolding of these basal concepts a certain use of symbolism has become necessary. But the discerning reader will penetrate the shell to the kernel that it conceals. In conclusion, I wish to disclaim any purpose to add another to existing systems of philosophy, of which the world is already over-full. My ambition is rather, through the emphasising of certain fundamental ideas, to impart a new spiritual vitality to the body philosophic. It is possible for philosophy to be spiritually dead while it is intellectually alive. But it is only through its spiritual energy that it is able to become an important organ of truth and to minister to the highest needs of humanity.

I wish to acknowledge the great debt I owe to my honored teacher, the venerable McCosh, to the spirit of whose realistic philosophy I hope my own work will be found to be loyal. My acknowledgments are due to Mr. A. L. Frothingham, Sr., of Princeton, for important suggestions regarding the principle of dualism and for kindness in reading and criticising my manuscript; also to my colleague, Professor A. F. West, for painstaking and appreciative interest in my work and for many helpful criticisms and suggestions, and to my pupil, Mr. G. A. Tawney, for valuable assistance in reading proof-sheets. There are other obligations which cannot be acknowledged in detail. My indebtedness to the masters, Plato, Aristotle, Plotinus, Augustine, Kant, Hegel, and Lotze, is too obvious to require special mention.

ALEXANDER T. ORMOND.

PRINCETON, January 20, 1894.

CONTENTS

		PAGE
Introductory,		1
I.	The Norm,	9
II.	Being and Non-being,	24
III.	Becoming,	44
IV.	Space and Time,	59
V.	Cosmic Nature,	70
VI.	Organic Nature,	83
VII.	Psychic Nature,	96
VIII.	Consciousness,	115
IX.	Morality,	125
X.	Non-being and Evil,	138
XI.	Communal Nature,	155
XII.	History,	171
XIII.	Religion,	194
XIV.	Art,	218
XV.	Knowledge,	235
XVI.	Logos,	255
XVII.	God,	266
XVIII.	Spiritual Activity,	292
Conclusion,		300

BASAL CONCEPTS IN PHILOSOPHY

INTRODUCTORY

ONE of the most striking features of contemporary thought is its weakness in respect to fundamental philosophical conceptions. The masses of the intelligent are espousing agnosticism, not as the result of any reasoned conviction, but out of sheer inability to rise above the middle axioms of human thinking. To this weakness is due in great measure the prevalence of sensationalism in Psychology and phenomenism in Philosophy; the former springing out of a kind of blindness of the soul to its own spiritual nature; the latter from the inability of the reason of the time to conceive any categories of reality transcending the mechanical and sensible.

It is the merit of the transcendental movement, in the thinking of this century, that it possesses an insight which leads it to refuse to respect the limits of phenomenism and to insist not only on the existence of realities beyond the sensible horizon but also on the power of human intelligence to embrace these within the circle of knowledge. But transcendentalism, although it has the root of the matter in it, has not been able to wage on the whole a successful warfare against superficial tendencies. Kantism has failed on account of its only partial grasp of the conditions of its problem and its consequent aloofness from the processes of experience, while Hegelism, a much more competent theory, and one that has in it the true antidote of phenomenism, fails in part, because of its misconception of the true dialectic of spirit, a misconception that leaves the system prisoned in a closed sphere of absolutism. The clash of philosophical systems is thus reducible to a conflict between speculative blindness on one side, and a kind of speculative aberration on the other, with no competent mediator in sight to heal the breach.

Again, the trend of the scientific thinking of the century has been so strong in the direction of evolution that faith in it has come to be a recognized test of scientific orthodoxy; while, on the other hand, the religious orthodoxy of the time has felt constrained to take toward the evolution theory, if not an attitude of hostility, at least one of distrust, on account of its tendency to unsettle religious convictions and its apparent hostility to supernaturalism and the doctrine of final causes. A painful breach has thus arisen between the convictions of science and those of religion, and this breach has contributed still further to cloud the vision and to trouble the spirit of the time.

The following inquiry is an attempt to deal with

these and other scarcely less grave issues in a way that will not be open to the charge of superficiality. We are convinced that the only radical cure for the limitations of our thinking is to be found in the discovery of profounder and more adequate categories. Knowledge is founded in categories, and its successive stages arise not primarily, out of the generalization of facts, but rather out of the emergence of new categories under which our generalizations are to proceed. We not only generalize facts, but our reflection rises from categories of space and time to those of substance and cause, and only rests finally in the supreme ideas of unity and ground.

Now when we seek to construe the ground of things adequately we are led by a necessary trend of reflection to translate it into the self-existent, and this again into the self-active energy of Aristotle. But self-activity in itself does not afford a final resting-place for thought. Consciousness is either a mere by-product and spectator in the universe, or it is inherent in the primal essence of things. But self-consciousness is a form of self-activity and cannot be conceived as a by-product. And all consciousness is going on to be self-conscious. The final resting-place of thought is found when self-activity and self-conscious activity are identified, and primal being is translated into conscious self-activity.

When primal being is conceived as conscious self-activity its highest category can no longer be the logos construed as abstract intelligence. The reflection of Anaxagoras and Aristotle is not adequate on this point, but we must learn the lesson of the subsequent historic movement which culminated in the idea of the logos as a principle of immanent personal activity. And if the objection be raised that such a conception of the logos could not be completely attained without reference to religious history and literature, we would meet the objection with a plea of confession and avoidance. Philosophy must recognize its indebtedness to history, and especially to religious history. The highest spiritual intuitions of the race have been achieved through channels of religious experience. We claim for philosophy the right to seek light wherever it can be found. If this light should come through the channels of sacred literature, that is no reason why philosophy should not avail herself of it, provided she do not receive it on mere authority, but is able to translate it into rational terms and deal with it according to her own legitimate methods.

The logos is the highest category of rational insight, and when applied to the primal self-activity renders a conception of its nature possible. In short, the cure of the agnostic blindness is to be found in the logos-category. This renders the immanent nature and activity of absolute being intelligible. In its light we are able to conceive a spiritual movement of internal conscious distinction and unity, which translates the Absolute into living spiritual energy and personal being. And this achievement not only intelligizes the ground of reality but supplies the clew to its productive and generative relations to the world.

For it enables us to achieve an intuition of that primal dialectic of spirit out of which the whole generative movement of things proceeds. Here, as we see, one of the primal difficulties of reflection has arisen. The Hegelian insight has seized upon the dialectic, but has misconstrued it at a vital point. We must not only apprehend that the primal activity of being contains the dual moments of affirmation and negation, but we must also realize, as Plato did, that primal opposites can never pass into each other. Being, therefore, affirms itself, but it does not deny itself, but rather its opposite.

The problem of the negative becomes thus the last and most erudite issue in philosophy. If we yield the point that primal opposites may pass into one another, then the whole dialectic of reality becomes a process of the self-affirmation and self-denial of being, and the distinction between being and non-being vanishes. In that case, however, the dialectic is shorn of its power as an explanatory principle, for it can never render conceivable the generation of a relative order from the Absolute. Pantheism is thus its logical outcome.

If we maintain the position that primal opposites do not pass into one another, we then have the problem of non-being on our hands. For then spirit must be conceived as affirming itself, but as denying, not itself but its opposite. Non-being thus becomes a transcendent opposite to being, that which it negates, opposes, and seeks to suppress and annul. The value of this conception as an explanatory principle, as we find in the following inquiry, consists in the fact that it renders the genesis of a relative and imperfect order from the Absolute conceivable. That modification which differentiates the relative from its absolute ground becomes intelligible when we are able to supply a motive for creative energy and thus conceive a distinction between the immanent movement of spirit and its volitional outgo in creative and generative activity. This motive arises in spirit's intuition of its opposite, and its impulse to go out into what may be symbolically represented as the sphere of non-being, in order to annul the negative and generate positive reality in its place.

We admit that the doctrine of non-being thus arrived at is not free from difficulties. One of these arises from the necessity of conceiving non-being in a purely negative sense, and yet ascribing to it some of the functions of causation. This seems to involve a contradiction. We think, however, that the difficulty is greater in appearance than in reality. For it is conceded that effects in being may arise from the non-existence of positive conditions. Now, as the inquiry shows, the essential negative characteristic of the opposite of primal being is the absence from it of a ground or principle of self-existence. In view of this it may be symbolized as an abyss in which being has no support. A reality generated in such a sphere would participate in non-being in the sense that it would have no immanent principle or ground of self-existence. In this sense non-being is a cause in a purely negative sense and contradiction does not arise.

This absence of self-existence and this dependence on that which transcends it is, as St. Augustine profoundly shows, the differentia of relative and generated being. It is that modification which pantheistic principles are never able to explain, and upon which naturalism is ever stumbling into agnosticism.

The same principle, as the inquiry shows, enables us to attain a rational conception of the ground process of relativity, which is that of a passage from immanent potentiality to realized actuality, an evolution whose presupposition is a spiritual absolute, and whose stages are mechanism, life, and spirit. In the conception of the world-process thus achieved, there is a ground, we think, for the harmonizing of scientific and religious convictions. For if evolution be real and proceed according to the categories of mechanism and the law of natural causation, the basis of science is established and her intuition is vindicated; whereas, if mechanism and causality themselves have as their presupposition a spiritual absolute, and as their finality the evolution of spirit, the substantial requirements of the intuition of religion have been met and satisfied.

And this satisfaction will be the more complete if it is seen that out of the same grounds on which the whole historic process arises, springs also that principle of spiritual mediation which is one of the essential elements in religion. The whole spiritual history of nature and humanity finds its rationale in the postulate of a transcendent and self-existent being whose creative energy functions in the world as the immanent spiritual principle of its existence and development. This postulate grounds and rationalizes the whole realm of science and its categories, while in the sphere of the ultimate issues it provides, in the synthesis of immanence and transcendence which it implies, an adequate foundation for a Philosophy of Religion.

The spirit of the time is not lacking in scholarship or zeal for the truth. What it needs most is a fresh baptism in the fountain of insight. Philosophy needs to become more truly historical by escaping from the form and entering more into the spirit of the world's thinking. She must also use her own eyes to look up into the heavens and down into the heart of humanity. The organ of philosophy is reflection, but her highest gift is spiritual intuition. Through this she achieves the primal insight she needs to qualify her for her highest mission, which is to unify knowledge and heal the breaches of the human spirit.

I

THE NORM

Meditation on the history of thought leads to the conviction that Philosophy has a distinctive and individual norm, and that this norm contains in it the secret of the highest wisdom. But when we essay to search the annals of philosophy for the idea that will express its essence, we find ourselves launched on a perilous voyage over an uncertain sea. The highest point of ancient thinking was that reached in the speculation of Socrates, Plato, and Aristotle. At the heart of this reflection there functions an idea as the inner motive of its activity and development. The thought of Socrates is psychologic, and he conceives the idea as a principle of generic activity in the human consciousness. To stimulate this principle and develop from its activity a rational system of truth is the aim of all his teaching. Plato's thought transcends the psychologic sphere, and becomes ontologic. To his intuition the idea becomes transformed into an ontologic archetype, standing objective to conscious reason and energizing as the absolute formative principle in things. Aristotle's thinking is analytic and individual, and reacts from the transcendent universalism of Plato. The Stagirite attempts, and in a measure achieves, a reconciliation of the psychologic and ontologic points of view in his conception of the individual real as including, in one aspect, a synthesis of the universal and particular; in another, a union of self-activity and potence.

It is this latter aspect which is of interest here. Socrates had represented the idea as a self-active universal energizing in the consciousness of man, while Plato elevated it into a transcendent ontologic self-activity. Now Aristotle, in his distinction between self-activity and potence, achieves, what Socrates and Plato were not able to do, namely, a rational basis for a distinction between the primal ground of things and the nature of things themselves. The primal ground is pure self-activity, *purus actus*, while things are a dual synthesis of self-activity and potence. While, therefore, the primal ground is complete in itself, and is not moved, things have a history in space and time; they are not completely self-active but have a movement that depends upon conditions outside of themselves. Their history thus falls into a conditioned series, and evolution is their law.

The world's thought presents no deeper insight than this. Aristotle barely misses a final and adequate solution of the profoundest issue of philosophy. But the Aristotelian chain is not complete. The question still presses, If the primal ground of things be a pure self-active principle, why should not all the products of its energizing be the same? Why should potence and its fruit, imperfection, exist in a system whose creative springs are self-sufficient and perfect? To these questions this ancient speculation has no coherent answer. The modification of self-activity, which constitutes the differentia of produced things, is brought in by what Hegel would call an "external reflection," and is left without rational ground or explanation.

The scene of our meditation changes to the opening of modern speculation, and the vision of three epoch-making thinkers rises before our eyes. Des Cartes' thinking, like that of Socrates, finds its starting-point in the human consciousness, and the idea it develops is that of the psyche itself as thinking substance. But Des Cartes does not identify his substance with self-activity, conceiving it as relatively inert and motionless. His notion of the psyche turns out, therefore, to be speculatively barren, providing no adequate principle for rationally apprehending either God or nature, whose ideas are, nevertheless, inseparable from the human consciousness. The result is a practical failure of his enterprise and the breaking up of his system into a number of intractable and incommunicable spheres.

Spinoza is the Platonizing thinker of this group, who transforms Cartesianism into ontology by raising the uncreated substance of Des Cartes to the plane of absolute being, while he reduces the relative substances, mind and matter, to the ranks as the attributes through which it manifests itself.

But this ontologic transformation does not fully meet expectations. It vindicates the Absolute by swallowing up the relative, and with it the individual. Spinoza follows Des Cartes in his failure to identify substance with self-active principle. His absolute does not move, but stands there forever in the same place. *Natura naturans* is not a self-active being, a *purus actus,* nor is the *natura naturata* a manifestation of this self-activity in the forms of relativity. The relation is static, not dynamic. The primal substance is simply a substrate of attributes and modes which rest upon it, but are not rationally grounded in its nature. In Platonism we find a lower and a higher insight. When thinking in the lesser light Plato conceives the archetypes as mere models and patterns which an external demiurge dips into the material, so to speak, and forms created things. Under the influence of the larger insight, he rises to higher views and identifies the archetypes with self-active principles which operate as the formative energies of creation. Spinoza does not rise to this higher insight of the master. His system is Platonism on the lower plane of the archetypes, conceived after the analogy of the Cartesian substance and reduced to absolute unity. The pit of Spinozism is not pan-theism, but pan-substantialism. Its bane is its bondage to a false idea of substance, and its cure is to be found, not so much in the breaking up of its all-devouring unity as in the reform of its idea of substance.

In Leibnitz we find a reincarnation of the individualizing thought of Aristotle. Leibnitz has learned the fear of the all-devouring One of Spinoza, and the cure, he conceives, must be brought about by a reassertion of individualism. In his insight Leibnitz is a true child of Aristotle. He sees that philosophy has been bound and paralyzed by a false idea of substance, and he seeks to free her from her bondage by going back to Aristotle and restoring his doctrine of substance as a self-active principle. Under the double insight his reflection breaks up the ontologic unity of Spinoza into a plurality of self-energizing individual monads, potential or active spiritual psyches, each an independent substance in itself, because it contains in it the principle and motive of its own evolution. Leibnitz is also a true child of Aristotle in recognizing the limitations of pure individualism and in seeking to ground the finite, developing individualities in a "monad of monads," the equivalent of Aristotle's *purus actus*. In other words, Leibnitz's reform of the idea of substance is a revolution; it roots out the static conceptions which had dominated, and in a sense perverted, the early period of our modern thinking, and reintroduces into philosophy those dynamic categories under which the highest fruits of ancient speculation were achieved.

But in face of the highest problems of philosophy we do not find that Leibnitz is more successful than his master. To the question how the existence of the imperfect and undeveloped is consistent with the existence of a perfect self-active ground, Leibnitz has no rational answer. We look in vain in this modern cycle, as we looked in vain in the reflection of the ancient triumvirate, for a datum from which an intelligible reason for this emergence of imperfection from perfection can be deduced.

It is clear that our meditation must still go forward. For philosophy, as distinguished from psychology, the development from Locke to Hume has chiefly a negative value. It furnishes a natural history of the decline and death of speculation, smothered in a mass of empiric details. In Kant, however, the genius of philosophy again reappears. The Socratic thinking, modified by the Cartesian cycle, is again incarnated. Kant applies his analytic to human consciousness in order to rediscover in it those universals the loss of which had plunged British thought into scepticism. The result is the categories, the most important single outcome of modern philosophy. These categories are in the Kantian system the self-active universals which translate ordinary experience into rational knowledge and thus lay the foundations of science. But Kant, like Socrates, puts a psychologic limit on his categories; they are valid only for human cognition, but in the transcendent ontologic sphere are without authority. The result is that philosophy stands like a house divided against itself. Knowledge is only of subjective value while the shadow of an objective and transcendent Real forever haunts the consciousness of man and destroys his rest. Philosophy stands thus as a propounder of a sphinx's riddles and swallows up all her own children because they are unable to solve them.

Kant's failure was the motive of subsequent speculation. With a backward Dionysian sweep his negations fostered the agnostic tendencies of British thought. The forward impulse is toward transcendentalism. The transformation of the psychologic principle of Kant into ontology takes place in Fichte and Schelling. Fichte's reflection seizes on the shadowy noumenal self of Kant, which Kant had endeavored to secure in a moral postulate, and translates it into the idea of an absolute ego; while Schelling, rightly denying that Fichte ever completely succeeds in reducing the recalcitrant object or *Anstoss* to subjection to his absolute, conceives the project of enlarging the continent of being so as to embrace both subject and object in the notion of the Absolute. Schelling then completes the ontologic transformation of Kant in his dual conception of a transcendent absolute, in which subject and object, ideal and real, stand as parallels with a medial relation of indifference between them. But further reflection taught him at length that such a conception of the Absolute is self-contradictory, and that the real absolute in his system is the point of indifference itself; the evolution of which leads again into the closed circle of Spinoza, a fate from which he escapes only by losing himself in the clouds of theosophic mysticism.

In Hegel we have again a return from ontologic universalism to individualism. But the Hegelian return is on a higher plane than that of Leibnitz. To Hegel the individual is a category which contains in solution the universal and the particular, and from another point of view, the subject and object. Hegel's conception of absolute being is that of a self-active principle which includes the distinction of subject and object, and everywhere leads to individual manifestations. The self-activity of the Absolute expresses itself in a dialectical movement which passes through three stages in its return upon itself and functions everywhere as the inner reality of things. Now Hegel has two modes of conceiving the movement of this dialectic energy, (1) the logical, which starts with the most abstract notion of being and represents the dialectical procession of thought as a perpetual concretion which culminates in the highest and richest idea, that of absolute spirit; (2) the ontologic, which reversing the logical order starts from the idea of absolute spirit, and represents creation as the going out of absolute spirit into objective self-alienation, through nature and finite spirit back into itself. The process of relativity is thus conceived as a drama of self-evolution and self-reconciliation of the Absolute Spirit in which it is begun, continued, and ended.

Overawed by the magnitude of Hegel's idea our reflection might end here; but the old questions come up and clamor for an answer. We admit that Hegel has touched the highest point of modern speculation, but we are unable to conceive how logically a notion which is, *ex hypothesi*, the thinnest of abstractions (in Hegel being is the last abstraction) can be the bearer of a dialectic that presses on through self-affirmation and self-negation, never staying its footsteps until it has reached the bosom of absolute spirit. The truth is, the logical movement is a superinduction. The true dialectic is an external reflection; it is the movement of the spirit itself refusing to be satisfied until it has reached its own highest category.

The normal movement of Hegelism is the ontologic, the self-uttering of absolute spirit in the sphere of its manifestations. But here we meet a difficulty. How is it conceivable that absolute spirit can evolve or utter from itself anything less perfect than itself? We cannot conceive how absolute being, simply by an immanental dialectic, can generate from itself a sphere of relative and imperfect nature. There is no datum in Hegelism, as we found none in Aristotle, which makes it possible to ground rationally the distinctive character of the relative, or to justify the Absolute in resting satisfied with a relative and imperfect result of its energizing. And since this ontologic aspect of Hegelism is its side of chief philosophic value, we conclude that Hegel fails, as Aristotle failed and as Leibnitz failed, to discover a rational *nexus* between the relative and its absolute ground. The chasm still yawns before us, therefore, so that if we start from the relative we fail to reach the absolute ground; whereas, if we proceed from the Absolute, we are unable to find any real passage across to the sphere of relativity.

In the foregoing historical survey we have touched only the mountain-peaks of speculation, ancient and modern. The great lesson the masters have to teach is that philosophy reaches its highest category in the notion of being as, in its essence, self-activity. The intuition of this is as old as Socrates and Plato. In modern philosophy Hegel is the one thinker whose system has embodied the insight most clearly and adequately; and for this reason, in spite of all its shortcomings, Hegelism reaches the high-water mark of modern speculation. Its failure, therefore, to ground rationally the sphere of relativity in the Absolute has thrown modern thought back upon itself in a wave of philosophic despair. If the highest thinking fails to ground knowledge in an absolute principle, the logical inference seems to be that the attempt is vain and that agnosticism is the final outcome of philosophy.

Before accepting this conclusion as final, however, some further reflection is necessary. Let us assume that in the idea of self-activity philosophy has achieved its highest category. It is still possible for it to fall short in two distinct directions. It may either fail to conceive adequately the nature and implications of self-activity, or it may overlook some datum that is essential to the solution of its problem. The first of these considerations will occupy the remainder of this chapter. It will be conceded, we think, that a cardinal fault of old Platonism is its tendency to represent the self-active ideas or archetypes as independent entities, transcendent and objective to the mind of the Creator. And since these archetypes constituted the whole form and structure of rational conception and knowledge, a tendency inevitably arose in later Platonic thinking to separate the Creator from the world of forms and to regard him as only negatively conceivable, and therefore unintelligible. This tendency was stimulated by the contact of Hellenism with the pantheistic thought of the Orient, which forever oscillates between two poles; the negative unity of the absolute ground of the world and the nothingness of the sphere of plurality and change. An absolute cleft was thus threatened between the world and its creative ground. And for this difficulty there was no cure in the reflection of Aristotle. For while Aristotle espoused the doctrine of Anaxagoras and translated his *purus actus* into νοῦς or reason, this was conceived as abstract intelligence to which no definable internal character could be ascribed. This was but logical, since the Platonic ideas had been reduced to forms of relative existence, and no categories remained for the inner characterization of the Absolute.

Now, it was a consciousness of this widening breach, coalescing with a feeling of spiritual distance and alienation from God, that motived those mediational features which characterize the last efforts of ancient speculation. To this must be ascribed Philo's hierarchy of beings between God and matter, as well as that catena of emanations from the unthinkable One down to the plurality of the phenomenal world, which appears in the New Platonism of Plotinus and Proclus. The true speculative significance of these movements can be understood only when we connect them with old Platonism and the issue which it left open. For to this later reflection the self-active ideas to which the term reason, or logos, came to be applied, could not be left in their alienation, but they were seized upon and introduced as mediators between the Creative One and the created many. And in putting upon them this function they were also hypostatized and clothed with the attributes of quasi-personality. The intermediate natures in these later forms of Platonism are not abstractions or mere essences, but they are beings possessing some of the properties of personal agents.

The speculative genius of Christianity responding to a motive which was also active in these pagan systems, was able to take a great step in advance of their solutions. For while this pagan and semi-pagan thinking is able only to subordinate the logos to the Absolute One, and thus to heal the breach between it and the world in a merely external and mechanical way, Christian intuition takes a different road, and, denying the subordination and externality of the logos, conceives it as an immanent personal principle in the nature of the Absolute One. Thus understood, it becomes a medium in a double sense, (1) of the union and interaction between the Creator and the world, and (2) of the conceivability of the creative nature. For the gist of the Christian reflection is that reason cannot exist apart from personality, and that personality is an immanent category of the primal being. Personality is, therefore, the category that opens the nature of this being and translates into intelligible terms its relations to the world.

Modern philosophy has been largely blind to this result of early thinking, and the consequence has been general powerlessness in dealing with the ontologic side of the philosophic problem. But it has been reaching parallel results in the psychologic sphere. The almost irresistible trend of philosophy, since Kant, has been toward the recognition of self-activity as the highest psychological category. Kant's doctrine of the categories is gradually conquering the world. For we have only to construe these categories as self-active functions in order to recognize them as the analogues in the psychologic sphere, of the Platonic ideas. For just as in Platonism the ontologic elements were conceived as impersonal and external to the creative nature, so in Kantism the categories are regarded as impersonal functions external to the real personality of man. The trend of post-Kantian thought has been toward the reduction of these categories from their isolated position and the immanating of them in the constitution of a personal subject of experience.

If to the conception of self-activity which is developed in the movements sketched above we apply the historic designation logos, a term which the Stoics applied pantheistically to the divine world-energy, it may then be truly said that the profoundest activity of human thinking has devoted itself to the definition of the logos as the central category of reality. Early thinking, concerning itself chiefly with the ontologic problem, has in its efforts to reach an intelligible conception of the nature of primal being achieved the Christian idea of the Divine Logos, while modern thought, tracking up the same function of self-activity on the psychological side, has been gradually attaining to an adequate conception of the psychic logos or category of human personality. In both lines of reflection, the ontologic as well as the psychologic, the true progress of thinking has been in the direction of more adequate philosophic conceptions in the light of which self-active energy can be rationally conceived only under the category of the logos and as the nature of self-conscious and personal being.

In tending toward this result history only confirms the verdict of direct reflection. True psychologic insight shows that the primal root of personality is not to seek in the empirical stream of conscious states, but rather in that ego-principle which unifies the conscious life and gathers up the stream into the personal knot. Metaphysical reflection confirms the psychologic verdict, with its own insight into primal being as self-activity. It sees that self-consciousness cannot be denied to self-active being without contradiction, and that self-conscious self-activity *is* personal activity. The root of personal consciousness is thus to be traced to the self-active intelligence, and not primarily, as the Aristotelians have supposed, to the passive or purely empirical element in man's psychic nature.

Logos is construed here as the category of conscious personal self-activity.* The Stoics applied the term to the energizing principle of the world, which they conceived to be rational but impersonal. Here it is conceived to be the very principle and energy of personal consciousness. Being cannot render itself completely intelligible under the categories of substance or cause. It will not yield up its secrets if approached as abstract and impersonal intelligence. Neither is the Aristotelian insight, which saw in being a synthesis of self-activity and intelligence, altogether adequate. Being only becomes intelligible when we translate self-active intelligence into the energy of self-conscious personality.

* In the following discussions the term Logos is employed in two senses—(1), as above indicated, for the principle of personal self-activity; (2), for the personal manifestation itself. The context will indicate clearly enough in which sense the term is used.

II

BEING AND NON-BEING

1. Primal being is self-activity, and when viewed under the category of the logos it becomes self-conscious and personal. If we ask why it is necessary to conceive primal being as self-activity, the answer is that no other category is self-explanatory. Causality, for example, simply evades the philosophic demand by perpetually shifting the burden of explanation back upon a vanishing antecedent, unless, indeed, we translate causality itself into some form of self-activity. What is true of causality, holds of every other category. If, further, we ask why, having identified primal being with self-activity, it is necessary to conceive self-activity under the category of the logos, the answer is very much the same. Every idea of self-activity short of one which represents it as self-conscious, will be found to involve a subtle contradiction.

This is a hard saying. But self-activity is, in the last analysis, self-affirmation. We have also found it to be identical with *purus actus*, or being in which the highest possibilities are actual. Now self-conscious activity is to us the highest conceivable category. To suppose, then, that self-consciousness is not actual in the *purus actus*, is contradictory.

Moreover, if self-conscious, then personal, for personality springs necessarily out of being's self-recognition of self.

The logos is to be conceived as the principle of personality, and personality is self-realization. In order to grasp this clearly a distinction must be made between two things that are commonly confused—personality and individuality. If personality be definable as self-realization of self, then personality is internal to being and being may include a plurality of personal manifestations. But individuality is not internal to being. It is a comprehending unitary category which characterizes being as a whole. We moderns have to a degree confounded personality and individuality and have made the former do duty for the latter. This has worked to the detriment of clear thinking both in philosophy and theology. We broach no novelty in the concept of personality here advocated, but simply revive the dominating idea of the early thinkers of our era. These thinkers distinguished personality from individuality, and conceiving personality to be an immanent self-conscious process in being, saw no inconsistency in coupling the doctrine of the multipersonality of the absolute nature with that of its unitary individuality. If this early insight could be restored it would soon prove its value both for theology and philosophy.

The importance of the logos principle for philosophy arises partly from the fact that it breaks our bondage to external reflection, and giving us an insight into being enables us to identify our reflection with its own immanent movement.

From this internal stand-point we are able to conceive primal being, or the absolute ground of things, as a self-energizing nature, the form of whose activity is a circle of self-affirmation in which is eternally realized distinctive spheres of self-conscious and personal life. This internal activity of being received a notable representation in the reflection of the early Christian Fathers. Their motive was the desire to achieve a philosophical statement of the Christian idea of God, and in order to realize this they were led to seize upon the notion of immanent conscious self-activity as the germ out of which their doctrine of the Divine nature was gradually evolved. According to this mode of thinking God is not to be conceived as a motionless unity like the Oriental one, but rather as self-active being, the ceaseless pulsations of whose energy generate distinctive spheres of self-realization. Thus the primal or Father-nature is represented as generating a second nature, an *alter ego* or eternal Son. This is the Divine Logos which stands as the utterance or Word of the Father, and is thus a necessary medium for the going out of the Divine energy in the creation of the world.

But this creative logos does not complete the circle of the Divine energy. The creation is not at first an orderly and developed system, but rather a mass of unorganized and disorderly elements. Between this formless world and its author there is a chasm, and this dualism supplies the motive of a further impulse toward unification. Thus arises a third sphere of self-realization, that of the Holy Spirit, which is the necessary medium of the outgo of the Divine love into the world in order to bring the creature through a process of evolution into union with the Creator.

The full significance of this conception of the absolute nature does not reveal itself until we connect it with its presupposition; namely, that this nature can only be represented adequately under the category of self-active, self-conscious energy; that is, under the category of spirit. God is a spirit, and therefore he is eternally active, and his activity is perpetually realizing itself in spheres of personal self-manifestation in and through which it also comes into creative and organizing relations with the world.

There is, however, in this early thinking, an unreflected point, namely, the *nexus* or mode of connection between the Divine nature proper and the world. The immanent movement which this early intuition seized upon is a principle of absolute and perfect manifestation, but in itself it does not account for the rise of the relative and imperfect. This issue was partially obscured for Christian thought by the concrete solution of the problem which was embodied in the Christ as God manifest in the flesh. It did come up in the development of Christian dogmatics in the problem of the double nature of the Christ, which, while asserted, could not be conceived, and was, therefore, authoritatively affirmed as a mystery that transcends reason and can be received only by an act of faith. Now, outside of the early Christian reflection, the only thought of modern times that has reached this plane of speculation and the problems, which it presents, is that of Hegel and his school. The central idea of Hegel, as we have seen, is that of a self-active dialectic which constitutes the inner core and essence of being, and expresses itself in a self-realizing process, a going out and return upon self. Hegel is led, like the earlier thinkers, to conceive the primal nature as absolute spirit, and he represents the dialectic as passing through three corresponding stages, giving rise to a procession of Father, Son, and Holy Ghost. To Hegel's intuition the Father-nature as subject-spirit goes out and embodies itself in an object which, as such, is its negation or not self. In this stage of alienation and distinction it is the world, but in the moment of return into the bosom of the Father it is the eternal Son. Hegel thus, as Dr. Harris says, identifies the world with the second person of the Trinity. In the Hegelian as in the Christian intuition the mediation and unification of the world with God is the motive of a third sphere of personal manifestation, that of the Holy Ghost, the immanent spirit in the Divine evolution of the world.

Now, the unreflected point of the early thinking

has been reflected in Hegel, but not, we think, in a satisfactory manner. Hegel's solution of the knot consists in a *restoration of the negative as a necessary philosophic datum*. The world is the *other* of absolute spirit, and the other is realized through self-negation. That dialectic by which absolute spirit traverses the circle of personal manifestations contains in it the moment of negation. In going out from itself it *others* itself, and this other is its negative or not-self. The not-self is the world, and thus the world and its process are mediated by negation.

Philosophy made a great stride in this thought of Hegel. But it has not, we think, reached a final solution of the issue involved. For the immanent negation by which being is translated into its other does not break the link of its self-identity. The *other* is, therefore, the *same* as being, only in an objective form, and must, therefore, be as absolute and as perfect as being. Being cannot by self-negation reduce itself from the plane of perfection to that of the relative and imperfect. Hegelism supplies no rational grounds for the modification which takes place in the character of being in its translation from the absolute ground, to the world, and for this reason it has not achieved a final solution of its problem.

In the preceding chapter we pointed out that philosophy might fail either through an inadequate conception of its categories or by neglecting to take into account some necessary datum. The failure above indicated seems to arise from the latter cause. Both the early and the later thinking break down at the same point. They fail to make it conceivable how the immanent activity of an absolute nature can give rise to a sphere of relative and imperfect manifestation. The first step toward the solution of the difficulty must be sought, we think, in a denial that the dialectic of being has been adequately conceived. In order to make this denial good it will be necessary to retrace the steps of the dialectic through which the personal distinctions in the absolute nature are conceived to arise. Following the line of Hegel's reflection we see how the self-manifestation called the Son or logos arises. But the logos does not present itself as the *objective other* of the manifesting nature, but rather, to take an analogy from the ego in the human consciousness, it stands forth as the uniting idea or self-conscious manifestation of the primal self. This ego is not the object of the primal self in the sense that it is its *not-self*, but rather in the sense that it is its *alter ego*. Now there is a negative movement which arises at this point. The ego consciousness arouses, by a necessary reaction, the antithetic consciousness of its opposite or not-self. The consciousness of the not-self is, thus, a function of the primal self, but the *not-self which it intuits cannot in any sense be conceived as identical either with the primal self or its realized other*. It is excluded from both, and is their object in the sense of being their qualitative opposite. In like manner, in connection with the logos-consciousness of the absolute, we must conceive that there springs up by a necessary negative movement, the consciousness of the *a-logos* as its antithetic opposite, and, therefore, excluded from it. The object which thus arises cannot be in any sense identified with either the Father nature or the logos, but is to be conceived as an outer sphere of antithetic negation. The mistake that reduces Hegelism to illusion at this point may be stated as follows: Hegel, following the train of Plato's reflection in the Sophist, conceives that the distinction between opposites is only relative and that they may pass into each other. But Plato plainly indicates that in his whole discussion of being and non-being he has the problem of classification or the basis of genera and species in view, while to the question whether there be an absolute opposite of being he has long since said good-by.* Now it is precisely this question of the opposite of absolute being on which Hegel is engaged. But it is clear that while the opposite of any species of being may be a species of being, the opposite of absolute being cannot be any species of being. The opposite of absolute being must be the negative of its being and must, therefore, be non-being, and it is contradictory to conceive that being and non-being can pass into each other. Our intuition will be *rectus in curia* only when we see clearly and cling to it, that there can be no passage of primal opposites into each other. The primal negative of being is non-being, and this non-being must be conceived as a

* The Sophist, Jowett's Translation, Ed. 3, vol. iv., p. 394.

datum that ever confronts the intuition of being, and which being ever strives to cancel and annul. Only so does the negative become a real datum in philosophy, supplying a negative ground of the differentia of relativity as well as a motive for the outgo of the energy of creation.

We have, then, the intuition of an absolute nature which by its inner dialectic activity, not only develops a conscious embodiment of the logos or *alter ego*, but through it also a consciousness of an antithetic *other* which negates its whole sphere of being. To this antithetic other the term *non-being* may be applied, and we thus arrive at the notion of the Absolute as becoming conscious through its logos-consciousness, by a negative movement, of an *a-logos*, or outer sphere of non-being.

In the idea of non-being we find a key to a problem that has hitherto baffled solution. That problem is the genesis of an imperfect and relative order from an absolute ground. To the question why the world should not be perfect, if it be grounded in absolute being, philosophy has had no answer. The answer here given is that the world is not to be conceived as the immediate product of the immanent energy of the Divine, but rather as its mediated product. The mediating term is non-being. The world can be produced only by the outgoing energy of the logos and only in the sphere of non-being and not in God. There is thus an element of nothingness constitutional to things, and this accounts for that modification which in the process of being created, renders things mutable and imperfect.

That non-being is a *real* datum, is a conception which philosophy finds great difficulty in realizing. Plato in the "Timaeus" has an intuition of it in his idea of ὕλη or matter. But his insight halts, and he conceives the negative sometimes as the mere receptacle of being and again as the mother of generation. In the first point of view he represents it under the analogies of space; under the second he conceives it to be a kind of material matrix in which the elemental forces, fire, air, water, and earth are generated and enter into the constitution of the soul as disturbing elements, of temperament and passion. Alexandrian Platonism identified non-being with the corporeal and the corporeal with evil. Hence arose its determined hostility to the Christian doctrine of the Incarnation and its decided trend toward asceticism. Christianity avoids this extreme while recognizing the dualism between good and evil in the spiritual world, and identifying evil with negation. St. John has an intuition of the cosmic significance of non-being in the glimpse he gives of the drama of creation, and the darkness and chaos standing over against the light-giving Logos. But in the earlier stages of the post-Apostolic movement, the speculative genius of Christianity was largely absorbed in the development and formulation of its conception of the Divine nature, in the course of which the gnosis of the negative was, for the time, left relatively in the background.

The speculative motive for again bringing it forward was introduced largely from the outside. Manicheism, which was an offshoot of Parseeism, and supposed to have been founded by Manes, one of the Persian Magi, had spread extensively over the East and ultimately came into contact with Christianity, upon which an effort was made to graft its leading tenets. The central idea of the system is that of an absolute spiritual dualism between two independent, coördinate, and antithetic deities, the Prince of Darkness and the Prince of Light, who engage in an eternal struggle for supremacy. Around this central core was aggregated a body of doctrines which were for the most part irrational if not immoral.

The historic importance of Manicheism for modern philosophy arises almost wholly from St. Augustine's connection with it, who for a time an adherent of the system, at length rejected it and reacted violently against it. But Augustine, although he threw off Manicheism, was unable to throw off the problem which it propounded, the relation of negation and evil to God or the Absolute. We find in Augustine the fruitful beginning of a real gnosis of non-being. Running through his refutation of the Manicheans, and his great work *De Civitate Dei*, is a current of rich speculation which culminates in that consummate flower of early Christian reflection, "The Confessions." The "high argument" reaches its climax in Book XII of *De Civitate Dei* and in Books XI and XII of "The Confessions."

Augustine rejects the Manichean doctrine of the

positive nature and eternity of evil. It has its actual origin in the will of the creature. All wills are primarily good. Evil originates when the creature turns from God and chooses some lower good. Augustine distinguishes between positive and negative causes and conditions, and contends that it is folly to ask for a positive cause of an evil will. The positive antecedent of a bad will is a good will. The good will is not the cause of the evil will. Evil is the turning of the will from the supreme Good; it has no positive cause outside the will that thus turns. The evil will has, however, a *negative* condition, and that is the *mutability* of the creature. This mutability is the differentia of creature existence and it has its ground in the *nothingness* out of which the creature is made. Augustine, in his doctrine of creation, opposes both old Platonism, which posited a primary matter, and Neo-Platonism, which taught the emanation of the world from God. Against these he develops his theory of creation out of nothing. Now in his whole reflection it is plain that Augustine's mind oscillates between two inconsistent conceptions of this nothing. The view which he verbally espouses is that which perpetuated itself in later theology, and which takes nothing as absolutely identical with unreality. But the assertions which he makes about the nothing are consistent only with its negative reality. God did not make things out of himself or out of eternal matter, but out of nothing. The assertion "out of nothing" would be wholly inane if nothing were not conceived as entering in some way into the nature of the creature. Again, in connection with his theory of creation the problem of evil and its relation to God comes up. God is not the author of evil. The creature is *mutable* because he is made out of *nothing*, but things may be mutable and good. Mutability is not evil, but it introduces into a nature the liability to evil, since through it contingency affects the will, in that the creature having the option of the supreme Good or the nothing, before it, may choose the nothing for its good and thus become evil. The trend of Augustine's real thought is toward the conception of evil as real though negative, and, in like manner, toward the conception of the nothing which is its negative condition as a negative reality. In other words, to the thought of Augustine the nothing is a datum which explains something, whereas the conception of it that got lodged in subsequent theological thinking is not a datum and is powerless to explain anything.

The survival of Augustine's verbal doctrine of the nothing which identifies it with the unreal was followed logically by two unfortunate results. The first was the giving up of the whole problem of creation as an unthinkable mystery. If the nothing is to be identified with mere unreality, then the proposition that God made the world out of nothing, can only mean that there existed no external motive or datum for the creation, and that the motive and data of the world must be sought wholly within the Divine nature. The difficulty is not escaped by ascribing the origin of the world to a fiat of a Divine will. A fiat of will accomplishes nothing unless it be accompanied by energy. Even on the fiat theory it is the Divine energy that is the producing cause. Why, then, should we not say that God created the world out of himself? This question is unanswerable unless we acknowledge the reality of the nothing. Rationally the only alternatives are the recognition of the reality of non-being or the surrender of the whole problem of the origin of the relative to the agnostic.

The second unfortunate result has been the giving up of the problem of evil as an unsolvable riddle. We must regard evil as either positive or negative. If we conceive it to be positive, then we are driven either to the Parsee dualism, if we regard good as also positive; or to pessimism, if we conceive good to be negative. If, on the contrary, we conceive evil to be negative and identify negation with unreality, we cannot but regard evil as unreal. This is the metaphysical assumption underlying all optimistic or other theories which conceive evil to be the mere privation of good, or good in the making. No theory of evil can be adequate that does not regard it as both negative and real. But unless negation is real this cannot be.

We may try to escape these subtleties by seeking the source of evil in free will, and for this we have the example of Augustine. But unless we recognize the reality of non-being or the nothing, we can find no refuge in free will, for the question confronts us, why should free will be contingent if the freedom of the Absolute does not constitute liability to evil? Augustine was able to point to the nothing out of which the creature is made as constituting the ground of his mutability and the consequent contingency of his free will; and so must we if our explanation is to have any rational force. But we then raise non-being into a real datum which explains something. There is no escape; either reality of non-being or a choice between a one-sided pessimism or optimism, or else the surrender of the whole problem as an unsolvable riddle.

A philosophy that goes to the root-problems must face the negative. It will have not simply the problem of being but also that of non-being on its hands. The crucial questions regarding the negative will be how its reality and its primal relation to absolute being are to be conceived. Now, as we have maintained, the reality of non-being does not carry with it the supposition that it is any sort of a positive nature. This has been the mistake of Platonism, which identifies the negative with matter, or at least, with space; also, of those modern systems which either conceive an abyss out of which both being and the negative arise, or, represent the negative as a hostile potency in the absolute nature which has only to be liberated from the bond of the absolute will in order to develop actual disorder and evil. Non-being cannot be conceived as any kind of activity, or as a potency out of which anything develops. It has no type and can be represented by no positive, constructive categories. It negates all positive predication. The only guiding clew we can have to its characterization is that of antithesis and opposition. It is what being excludes from its nature as contradictory. Shall we call it energy, or cause, or substance? By no means. It is the negation of all these. It is the negation of energy in that so far as it enters as a datum there is a failure of energy to do work. It is the negative of cause in the same sense as Augustine conceives mutability to be the negative cause of evil; not a generator of evil but the root of that contingency which makes a will liable to evil. It is the negative of substance in that it has no positive principle of existence in itself. It lacks the spring of self-evolution and self-perpetuation, and being the negation of these, it is the root of that mutability, that lack of self-subsisting activity, which constitutes the differentia of all creature existence.

That the assertion of the reality of non-being is not open to the charge of absolute dualism, and that it is a very important and necessary philosophical datum, the following statement will serve to show. Absolute dualism is a theory of the Parsee type which splits being into two antithetic halves, thus breaking its unity and perpetrating the same kind of an error in philosophy that polytheism is in the sphere of religion. But absolute dualism arises only when being is cleft, and positive, active, and co-ördinate principles are arrayed in antagonism to each other. It is needless to say that no such dualism is involved in the theory of non-being set forth above. In the first place, the whole conception is arrived at by the use of a unitary principle, the logos, for the interpretation of absolute being. The result of this step is the conception of absolute being as spirit which expresses itself in self-conscious personal self-manifestation. Absolute being is thus a necessary presupposition of non-being, and being itself is one. Its unity is not broken.

Thus the first presupposition of the real is being. Now the intuition of non-being arises out of the spiritual dialectic. That same movement of intellection which reveals being to itself, also confronts it with the intuition of the not-self, an object which in the absolute sphere must be the negative opposite of being. The root of the dual intuition is thus found in the heart of being itself. The negative intuition which arises is simply the negative aspect of reality, which is qualitatively opposed to being and excluded by its positive nature.

Now, that this negative is not to be conceived as internal and immanent to being is evident from the fact that it is being's opposite, *i.e.*, that which being denies and excludes from itself. The relation is one of primal opposites which, as we maintain, can never be conceived as passing into one another without gross confusion of thought. Negation as an activity is always being's denial of its opposite, and negation as the object of denial is always being's opposite. There is no self-negation of being, but what being negates is its opposite or non-being.

This is absolutely true in the sphere of the Absolute. Qualification is only necessary for the relative.

Confusion on this cardinal point leads to the one-sided *Identitäts Philosophie,* as the Germans call it, which sacrifices distinction and difference to unity, and having in the ground of the system eliminated the distinction between being and non-being, is driven by an irresistible trend of logical necessity to its goal in a species of monistic pantheism in which the Absolute completely swallows up the relative.

Non-being as an objective and antithetic term in reality thus arises as a necessary consequence of being itself when conceived as spirit and construed in the light of the logos-principle. How, then, can the category of non-being be shown to be philosophically necessary? Its value arises chiefly as a principle of disjunction and discrimination. So applied it brings some vital philosophical conceptions to the birth which it would otherwise be very difficult to realize. In the first place it makes a disjunction between the immanent and the exeunt energizing of the Absolute not only conceivable but also rational, in the motive it supplies for it in spirit's intuition of its own negative and opposite. The very self-assertion of being which is its essence will lead it to assert itself against and upon its opposite for its suppression and annulment. In the second place, as we have seen above, a true conception of non-being renders the origin of the world-series and its relative character intelligible. The self-assertion of being against its opposite not only explains the exeunt energy but also the origin of the world-process, as not in the absolute but in the negative sphere. The negative sphere is being's opposite, and is negative in the sense that it lacks the ground-principle of self-existence which is the essence of being. Logically then, a creature originating in this sphere will be relative and mutable, its ground and rationale being not in itself but in another. In the idea of the negative we thus find the key to a problem over which all philosophy has puzzled; namely, how an absolute energy could produce a creature that is only relative. The outgoing energy can produce no other than a relative result.

The negative also renders intelligible the law of the relative sphere, which is upward development. If the world arises out of non-being and progresses toward being it follows that its process will be from the lowest categories, those which lie nearest to the nothing, through more advanced stages until it reaches its full development under the categories of spirit. From the material to the spiritual, from mechanism to teleology, is therefore the natural order of relative growth.

The nature and necessity of non-being thus become apparent. It is incumbent on philosophy then to assert the reality of both being and non-being; being as positive, self-subsistent, and self-active; non-being as being's qualitative opposite. The category of being is the logos; that of non-being the a-logos. Each is a necessary datum of reality; being, of its self-existent ground, its origin, positive nature, and development; non-being, of its mutability, its dependence on other, its tendency to disorder, dissolution, and death.

III

BECOMING

We think that a rational doctrine of Becoming is possible only in the light of the dual categories of being and non-being. In the preceding chapters we have investigated these, and have been led to the discovery of a necessary connection between them. We have seen that a true conception of being leads to the assertion of its negative and antithetic correlate, non-being; and that non-being cannot be conceived as an immanent movement merely, in the evolution of being. We have seen that if we conceive being as spirit, then non-being can be regarded only as its primal and excluded opposite, as that which it perpetually denies and annuls but never becomes identical with.

The category of reality is broader than that of being. The whole of reality has its negative side, and it is this negative side which being denies. The whole of reality cannot be being, for being is perfect and complete and could of itself supply no motive for the generation of the relative. Nor can non-being be conceived as internal to being, since non-being is negation and want and being cannot be affected internally by these. The activity of being is, as we have seen, a dialectic in which spirit affirms itself, and denies and negates its opposite. Being never denies itself, but it denies and seeks to annul the whole negative aspect of reality. The processes through which this annulment is realized will, therefore, not be immanent, but will have their existence in the negative sphere of reality. Non-being is thus the negative side of reality and is itself real. It is the primal opposite of being, that which being denies and annuls. In this qualitative sense it is external and alien to being, a term which must be overcome and suppressed in order that being may be realized.

How, then, shall the category of non-being be conceived and made available for philosophic reflection? It cannot be conceived literally as antagonizing the energy of being, for it would then be transformed into a kind of being. Nor can we conceive it simply as the non-existent, since the non-existent is also supposed to be unreal. Non-being has no categories of its own, since all categories primally belong to being, and in the strictest sense it is, therefore, unrepresentable.

We have seen, however, that non-being is a necessary datum, and in order that philosophic thinking may get on, it is necessary that there should be some mode of representing it. Now, the negative is to be conceived as the opposite of being in the sense that it is what being denies and annuls. This relation will enable us to represent non-being symbolically by simply applying to it the negatives of the categories of being. If, then, we conceive being to be a sphere of reason, consciousness, light, order, personality, and individuality; non-being will be representable as the opposites of these, unreason, unconsciousness, darkness, caprice, impersonality, and dividuality. If we conceive being to be creative, generative, formative, and constructive; non-being will be representable as decreative, degenerative, deformative, and destructive. If we conceive being as energy that makes for ideal truth, beauty, and good, non-being will be representable as the negative ground of falsehood, deformity, and evil. It is only necessary thus to unfold completely the idea and categories of being in order to reach an adequate negative conception of non-being. Non-being is irrational, unconscious, dark, chaotic, impersonal, and dividual. It is decreative, degenerative, deformative, and dissolutive. It is the negative principle of falsehood, deformity, and evil. Exercising the philosophic imagination we may represent it as an abyssmal gulf of darkness and caprice eternally confronting the Absolute intuition in opposition to his creative energies.

We must not, however, in thus characterizing the negative allow our terms to mislead us. Non-being is a necessary datum of reason and an element in reality, but it is not representable to the imagination except symbolically. Nor can we apply to it any category in the positive, that is, in the active sense. If we conceive it under the category of cause, as we must, our term cause must be used in the negative sense. It is not the active generator of the properties of things which it is necessary to explain, but rather their negative condition. Want and negation are negative but not positive causes, and non-being is a cause in that it is a metaphysical want in the nature of relativity. For since the relative arises in the negative sphere, its self-existent ground will not be in it but in another. In this sense, non-being is a negative cause.

We think it important that philosophy should achieve this idea of negative causation, for it represents the only practicable mode of characterizing the negative element in reality. It is only when non-being is conceived as negative cause, that the mutability of generated things and their dependence on other can be understood, and it is only when we become able to apply this mode of characterization with insight and discrimination that we can avail ourselves of the true riches of the negative.

The question then arises, how are we to employ the dual categories, being and non-being, as data for a theory of becoming. The first three categories of Hegel's Logic are being, nothing, and becoming. But Hegel identifies being with the thinnest abstraction; *i.e.*, the real disrobed of every definite and positive attribute. This renders being indistinguishable from nothing, since both are represented under negative conceptions. Hegel is only logical, therefore, when he translates the negative movement of the dialectic into being's denial of itself and the whole activity of being is thus conceived monistically as immanent self-evolution. The reform which we think necessary is that the dialectic be dualistically interpreted and that non-being be conceived not as being in the form of negation, but rather as the primal opposite of being, which being denies and annuls. The dialectic of being and non-being, in so far as it is real, must be construed as an outgo of being's energy into the negative sphere of reality, and its activity will be an activity of opposition.

This substitution of a dualistic for a monal conception of the dialectic of being works a complete revolution in it while preserving and in fact increasing its unique suggestiveness and power. So conceived, it becomes an activity in which being as self-active spirit, realizes intellectually in its first motion, a dual intuition of itself and its negative opposite. This intuition motives a volitional movement which is to be conceived as the creative impulse of being, embodying itself in the outgoing of energy into the negative sphere. The result of this volitional onslaught upon non-being is creation, the generation of a positive nature in the sphere of want and negation. In this generated nature we have the origin of the species of reality we call becoming. How then shall the nature of becoming be conceived. In seeking an answer to this question, we must again revert to the antithetic data out of which it has arisen. Following the line of reflection opened by the early thinkers and developed by Hegel, we have conceived the world as the product of the volitional energy of the creative logos, while its evolution is the function of absolute energy conceived as Holy Spirit.

The question arises why this distinction is to be made between the energies of creation and evolution. The answer will be found in two considerations. In the first place, while the Absolute is to be conceived as spirit, its primal activity must be intellectual, and thus will arise the dual intuition of self or being and of the negative or non-being. This will lead by close sequence to the second moment of activity, which is volitional and presupposes the intellectual intuition as its motive. The volitional activity, as we have seen, asserts itself transitively in the energy of creation. The Absolute conceived as thus energizing and motived by the intellectual intuition is the creative logos. We see then that the same reflection which leads to the idea of the volitional activity also assigns to it the function of creation.

In the second place we have seen how the creature which arises from the creative energy is generated, not in being, but in the negative sphere. A form of being thus arises out of non-being. This determines the generation as beginning with the lowest categories and the creation will be, in its initial stage, next to nothing, and thus removed as far as possible from the Absolute. This distance between the creature and the Creator will motive a third activity of spirit in which it goes out into the created sphere in an energy of unification and love. The process which results from this unifying activity is development or evolution. It is a deep insight that applies the name Holy Spirit to the primal being in the exercise of this activity of development. The inner core of holiness is an activity of unification leading to the realization of wholeness or unity of being and the beauty of its manifestation. Thus arises what in theological language is called the procession of the Spirit, or in Scriptural phrase the moving of the Spirit upon the face of the deep. And this moving of the spirit is the immanent principle of the world-process, including both nature and humanity. It is true that nothing is made without the logos. It is also true that the unifying spirit is the immanent agency in the historic evolution of the world.

To the generated sphere conceived as the product of the logos and as motived by the spirit, we apply the name becoming. The term is suggestive of the flux of Heraclitus, and it may be conceived under the figure of a flowing and ebbing stream. Becoming is not pure being, nor is it pure non-being, but it participates in both, and thus its nature represents a dualistic synthesis. The idea of becoming involves dual and opposite tendencies to being and to non-being. The Heraclitean intuition had the keener sense for the negative side. The flux thus became a species of non-being and sceptical despair was the logical result. But becoming is as truly a tendency to being as to non-being. The energy that generated it continues, as we have seen, as conserving and developing force, and thus determines the positive moment of becoming not only as real, but also as dominant, so that negation becomes a subordinate and not a ruling feature in the system of things. While, therefore, becoming in its ground-constitution is dualistic and its activity expresses itself in a perpetual oscillation between the positive and negative poles of reality, the immanent energy of the Absolute conserves the positive forces and translates the flux into a movement of development from lower to higher stages of reality.

It is only in the light of this metaphysical duality that we can arrive at a completely rational conception of the nature of becoming. This major dualism is necessary to explain (1) the form of relative being; (2) what may be called the complemental duality of its constitution. Becoming is, as we have seen, dual in its constitution; it is a perpetual flux which is determined by opposite moments of generation and decay. Now, what is the meaning of this duality of form? It signifies that the relative is not a pure creature of absolute energy, that it cannot be monistically explained. The secret of its dual character is to be found in the fact that it is the generated product of energy that works in the negative sphere, and produces being out of it by the suppression and annulment of the negative. But this war against non-being is endless, and the negative enters as a moment into generated being, rendering it mutable, dependent, and contingent to decay.

We find here also the key to another feature of the relative; namely, the complemental duality of its constitution. In a self-conserving, self-subsisting medium a dual balance of forces would not be needed. But in the negative sphere from which the self-existent ground is absent, a generated force cannot be self-conserving, but must be conserved by its other or fall into the abyss. The only mode in which a relative nature can be conceived as obtaining a ποῦ στῶ is that of a complemental dualism of positive forces. This complemental dualism of forces, which, as we see, is not ultimate, but presupposes the Absolute, is the ground of a universal law of relativity; namely, that of *relative self-maintenance*, which has an application to both matter and mind.

Limiting our view to the former, the most philosophical conception of matter is that which regards it as reducible in its ultimate analysis to dual centres of force. The conception of a material monad as the unit of material constitution, seems to be irrational and nugatory. It can only be asserted in a postulate that can give no rational account of itself, and it holds in it no principle that can help us to rationally conceive its own persistence, or that can explain any of the characteristic material phenomena. If we posit the monad, it is necessary for us immediately to give it a fellow, held in the grip of a cohesive and repellant synthesis, before we can take a single step forward. This indicates that the rational unit of matter is the duad and not the monad. It is upon the duad only that mechanical science can rise, and a metaphysic of matter lay its foundations.

Assuming the material duad and the law of self-maintenance involved in it, let us consider the basal category of the relative process; namely, the Series. Reflection here will lead to analogous conclusions. The metaphysical dualism of being and non-being out of which the relative arises, can give rise to no series unless we conceive the complemental duad as the type of relative being. For we have seen that the mere notion of a dialectic of being and non-being leads to the intuition of a flux, a mere succession of sparks, an alternation of origination and cessation. Decay, dissolution, and death are as real as their opposites; they are ever present moments in the relative, constituting the negative ground of its mutability and dependence. But the moments of origination and cessation do not constitute the series. The principle of conservation in the Absolute is self-subsistence, self-identity, while its opposite in non-being is absolute discontinuity, and dividuality. In such a sphere the relative analogue of absolute self-subsistence can only be a succession of pulsations in which the energizing centre of the expiring pulsation persists and passes into its successor. This persistent core is to be identified with the spiritual potence in the form of which the immanence of the absolute energy in the world is to be conceived. Thus the series arises, a synthesis of opposite moments. The series may be conceived either as discontinuity ever striving to make a breach in continuity, or as continuity striving to heal the breaches of the discontinuous. The series expressing itself in the category of *change* is a dual alternation of cessation and origination in which a dialectic core of being persists.

The series thus realizes the law of self-maintenance, and this law, conceived as the inner principle of the series, is Causality. Here the same fundamental moments appear. The profoundest science of the time reduces the category of cause, on one side to the universal law of conditions; that is, the principle by which all phenomena are connected in an order of dependence; and on the other, to the law of dynamic continuity; that is, the principle by which the change from cause to effect is conceived to be only a change of form, in which the substance continues the same. Both these lines of conceiving state the same ultimate fact, the dualistic nature of the principle of causation. The first point of view, confining itself more rigorously to the sphere of manifestation, simply embodies in its concept of causation the inner nature of the series; whereas the latter more profoundly transcends serial limits of manifestation, and connects the changing series with its ultimate dialectic core. But this profundity, instead of transcending the sphere of dualism, simply leads to the "hidings of its power," for analysis of the elements of the material continuity which is presupposed, only reveals to our intuition that ultimate dialectical opposition of being and non-being which underlies all relative nature.

We conceive that the idea of relativity unfolded above, supplies the only completely rational basis for a philosophy of nature. In the first place, it enables us to see that the real clash of thought in regard to the origin and history of the relative and finite is not between the concepts of creation and evolution, but rather between those of creative dualism and monistic self-evolution. All theories of the self-evolution of the world are monistic, and may be classed under two categories: self-evolution from either absolute being, or absolute non-being. Now, from the standpoint we have reached here we are able to see, as by intuition, that self-evolution from absolute being can never rationally explain the origin of relative and finite nature, nor can it give any intelligible account of its universally dualistic character. If the world is simply a self-evolution of absolute being, then the product ought to be absolute and no relative category ought to show its head. If nature is a self-evolution of absolute being, then nature ought to be a sphere of perfect freedom, and necessity could have no rational right to appear. The categories of relativity are wholly inexplicable from the idea of the world as a pure phenomenon of absolute being.

Even more powerless is the idea of self-evolution from non-being. This is the basis of the negative Dionysian theories and the theories of purely naturalistic evolution. To these the primal datum is some sphere of negative reality, the Dionysian theories conceiving the evolution of the logos out of the a-logos and relative nature out of the logos, while the naturalistic theories of evolution conceive the same process in materialistic terms. Naturalistic evolution postulates some primordial world-stuff transcending the categories of organization, and, therefore, a species of negative absolute out of which organized nature gradually emerges. Now, in order that this absolute world-stuff may supply a fruitful starting-point for development, it must be conceived as containing principles of organization in its bosom. But in that case the organizing principles become absolute, and the dual categories of being and non-being are acknowledged. Naturalistic evolution is thus forced, by the simple logic that order and form cannot be conceived as arising out of the orderless and formless, to the positing of absolute being as one of its necessary conditions.

The only species of monism that has any philosophic value is a monism that starts from the postulate of absolute being, and conceives the universe as being the product or manifestation of an absolute self-subsistent principle. The world is then represented as having the springs of its own being and evolution within itself, and its movements are all to be construed under the categories of self-manifestation and self-development. We are able thus to develop a concept of the evolution of absolute being, but we find our logic powerless to ground a real relative order, or to rationally interpret its dualistic character and categories.

Pure self-evolution is a category of absolute being and has no place in a sphere of relativity. Nor does it furnish any adequate explanation of the relative. If we start from it as the sole metaphysical datum, we are never able to bridge the chasm from absolute to relative, and if we seek to employ it as a relative principle, we then either elevate the relative into the Absolute by positing the primal springs of nature's subsistence within herself, or we form a closed circle of relativity which excludes the Absolute and has no rational ground.

We conceive, then, that the category of becoming is that of the whole relative sphere. Its presupposition is a metaphysical dualism of being and non-being. Out of this dual fountain issues the flux, the flowing stream, a creature that is ever coming into being and ever ceasing to be. This creature acquires relative stability through the complemental duality of positive forces which forms the type of a relative constitution, and stands as the analogue of self-existence in the Absolute. By virtue of its persistence it forms a series. The series is the form of the law of self-maintenance. Its inner principle is causality, and by virtue of its causal connections the dialectic core of being passes from moment to moment by change and development, and the sprouting of consequents out of antecedents becomes a law of the world's movement.

If now we apply the term *creation* to the generating process by which the relative is grounded, and the term *evolution* to the process of growth from antecedent to consequent which constitutes its order, then creation and evolution become complemental terms, and a complete theory of relativity will be seen to involve both.

IV

SPACE AND TIME

If the Absolute is a necessary postulate of the existence of things, non-being is a necessary postulate of their imperfection. No reason can be found in the nature of the Absolute why generated existence should be less complete and perfect than its self-existent ground. But a reason for this is supplied by the postulate of that which is qualitatively opposite to being. We have seen how the intuition of non-being arises and supplies a motive for the outgo of the creative energy of being into the sphere of its qualitative opposite. This determines the character of generated being in two ways: (1) the rise of things in the negative sphere determines them as contingent and mutable; that is, as lacking a ground or principle of existence in themselves; (2) the very necessity that creative energy should not remain immanent, but that it should go out or utter itself, is the reason for another essential characteristic of generated being.

The law of all utterance is that what is implicit in the uttering agent shall become explicit, and that what is explicit shall become implicit. To the utterer the thought is explicit and the symbol in which it expresses itself lies coiled up in its bosom. When it goes out into the outer sphere this order is reversed. The form uncoils itself and swallows up the thought, which becomes implicit as its inner energy and meaning. Thus the word is necessary to manifest the thought just as in Christian thinking the Divine energy utters itself in the eternal Logos.

This law is universal, and it involves an inversion of the categories of being in its outgo into the negative sphere. It is the operation of this law in connection with the modifying influence of the negative, as above explained, we think, rather than any labored effort to trace the moments of logical reflection, that will bring to light the real forms and energies of the world.

The most obtrusive elements of the world, as it presents itself to our cognitive intuition, are space and time and matter. Having treated of the genesis of matter in the preceding chapter, we shall devote this reflection to space and time. We must hold to the cardinal doctrine that the world has as its generating ground an absolute being; that this being is self-activity; and that self-activity is to be construed in the light of the logos, as spirit; that is, as self-conscious, personal, and individual. Self-activity is then an individualizing energy. It is an energy that is formally unitary, comprehending the whole and including distinction as internal and implicit.

The inversion of such an energy consequent on its

outgo or external utterance, would lead to a transposition of relations between its unitary and differencing activities. The latter, the category of dividuality, would become explicit and obtrusive, and the principle of its operation would be the distinction and expulsion of point from point, a process which is endless and to which no assignable limit can be fixed. The operation of such a principle would generate the relations of quantitative self-exclusion and externality. But the force of this dividual principle would be checked by the implicit unitary force of individuality which, when thus energizing in subordination to its opposite, would take the form of continuity. The quantitative points would thus fall into a species of dialectic, explicitly expelling, but implicitly comprehending all other points. Thus would arise that process of generation, that flowing out from points into lines, planes, and solids, which constitutes the central movement of all our space conceptions.

We have only to translate this supposition into fact in order to obtain a rational idea of the generation of space. For space *is* explicitly this principle of unchecked dividuality, this breaking up into an infinity of mutually expulsive points; this wholly outering and self-repelling property of reality. But space is implicitly individual and unitary, so that every point includes and comprehends all other points. The law of space conception is thus the evolution of point from point in the process which generates lines, planes, and solids.

How, then, is space related genetically to the self-active energy of the creative spirit? We answer, mediately, through the modifying influence of non-being. Space as above construed, is to be conceived as a first resultant in the negative sphere, of the outgoing creative energy. The first fruits of the outflow of the creative energy into the negative sphere, is its transformation into a quantitative image of its absolute author.

This we call ontologic space, and the question arises, what is the relation of ontologic space to matter? We cannot regard it as a phenomenon of matter, nor yet as separable from matter. In the order of conception it is the *prius* of matter. But on the other hand, we cannot conceive its existence apart from the existence of matter. We cannot separate what the Absolute has joined together. The true relation will, we think, be apprehended if we conceive space and matter as arising out of the same generative activity, space being its form while matter is its substance. Form and substance are inseparable, while in the order of conception, form must stand as the *prius* of substance. Matter and space, therefore, though not to be identified, are as inseparable as substance and form.

A distinction is to be made between ontologic and psychologic space. Ontologically considered, space is the form of matter. It is the principle of divisibility and continuity in the material sphere and is, therefore, objective and dependent on the creative energy that underlies the world. Psychologically considered, when we abstract from ontology, space seems to be subjective, a phenomenon of our perception. Kant conceives it to be the form of perception, and Berkeley virtually anticipated the Kantian view by reducing it to a perceptive process. The doctrine of the subjectivity of space contains both a truth and an oversight. The truth is that space is not to be conceived as a motionless thing lying wholly outside of the activity by which it is perceived. Berkeley and Kant are the authors of a real psychological discovery. We do not objectively contemplate space; rather, we spatialize objective phenomena, and the mode of this spatialization can only be adequately conceived when we regard it as analogous to the generation of ontologic space—that is, when we conceive our perception of phenomena *in* space as resulting from an inversion of the inner activity of the perceiving subject. Berkeley and Kant are following a deep insight, therefore, when they identify space with the form of external perception.

But the doctrine of these thinkers contains an important oversight. It does not take account of the objective factor, the ontologic conditions of perception. If we eliminate the objective factor, the incoming energy that meets the outgoing activity, we abolish perception. But if we recognize the objective factor, we have on our hands the whole ontological problem, and we cannot foreclose the case in favor of subjectivity, as these thinkers do, but must include the ontological as an integral part of our theory. When we do this, the intuition gradually dawns that, primarily, space is ontological and objective, and that in our psychological process we simply retrace the steps of a creative energy that has gone before.

The nature of time is to be analogously apprehended. The root of time, as of space, will be to seek in the nature of the creative activity. This activity, as we have seen, is one that is explicitly unitary and self-identical. But it implicates *change* in the form of immanent movement or procession, a movement which ever returns upon itself. Now, we have only to bear in mind the law of outer expression, to be able to conceive the expressed activity which goes out upon and in the negative sphere, as undergoing a transformation, so that the category of change has become explicit and obtrusive. The result will be parallel to that in the case of space. The moments of the inner activity which were all comprehended in an eternal consciousness will, through the transformation, have become explicit as a *succession* of moments or pulsations, each of which expels every other moment from itself. This will give rise to an indefinite plurality of moments which would be wholly disparate and disconnected, were it not for the fact that the self-identical activity, which in the Absolute holds the procession immanent, has now become implicit and functions as a principle of continuity. We have then a result analogous to that noted above. Explicitly, the moments are mutually exclusive and disparate, but implicitly each moment comprehends every other moment. The opposite characteristics of time thus arise, for time flows, but time is also continuous. Time is the principle of separate events, but it is time that binds events together in a continuous movement.

Thus arises ontologic time, regarding which we have to ask, as we asked regarding space, how are we to conceive its relation to the material world? In order to mark the distinction between matter, space, and time, which proceed from a common activity in the Absolute, we must note their variant relations to the sphere of non-being. The dual constitution of matter arises, as we saw, from the want of self-supporting ground in the negative sphere. The peculiar constitution of space arises from the dividuality of non-being, the absence from it of any principle of continuity; while that of time finds its negative condition in the chaos of non-being, the absence from it of any principle of orderly sequence. A cardinal point to be emphasized is that matter, space, and time have a common root in the Absolute; they spring simultaneously out of a common activity, and their differential features are the negative results of the medium in which they are engendered.

Now, we have seen that space is the form of which matter is the substance. How shall time be related to this complex phenomenon? In a preceding chapter we saw how the serial form of becoming originates. But the idea of time is also that of a series. Time bears the same relation to the series of becoming that space bears to matter. It is the *form* of the series, while its substance is that inner dynamic causal connection which, as we saw, constitutes the principle of natural evolution. The two ideas are inseparable, and when we say that the order of becoming is serial, we are also saying that it is temporal. The form of the series, time, and its substance, causal dependence, are thus inseparable, though not the same, and we are not at a loss to understand a tendency so marked in certain phases of modern thought, to identify the substance with the form, and to conceive causation in terms of pure temporal succession.

Time thus conceived, we call ontologic, because it has its roots in the creative activities which produce the world. This is to be distinguished from psychologic time, which arises in a way analogous to the rise of psychologic space, and regarding which the same problems have been mooted in modern thought. The solution of these problems need not delay us, since it is analogous to the solution of the space problems. It is true of time, that while it is to be conceived psychologically as the formal activity of the serial consciousness which apprehends events in succession, yet this subjectivity must be qualified by the recognition of time as springing from ontologic conditions, and, therefore, objective. In thinking time we retrace the pathway of the creative energy. Of the modern analyses of time, that of St. Augustine is the earliest and one of the most interesting. Augustine declines to regard the divisions of time into past, present, and future, as ultimate. There is in reality only the present, and there are three times, only in the sense of "a present of things past, a present of things present, and a present of things future." * Translating this into psychological terms, we have a memory-present, a sight-present, and an expectation-present. But when he comes to the analysis of this present which subserves everything, Augustine's insight fails and he confesses himself baffled.

Contemporary psychology is scarcely more successful in meeting the Augustinian difficulty. It distinguishes between a "specious present," which James picturesquely describes as "a sort of saddle-back with a certain length of its own, on which we sit perched and from which we look in two directions into time," and the real present, which forever vanishes to a point. This *real* present the psychologist finds inexplicable, and no wonder, for it involves a datum, we think, which transcends the temporal series. The objective life of man moves in a series, but there is a point at which it transcends the flowing stream and contemplates it forward and backward from the standpoint of eternity. It attains this point whenever it retreats into the citadel of the I. That intangible and indivisible present, which the keenest analysis of empiric consciousness never traces to its source, is the voice of the I, whose function, in relation to the temporal series, is to comprehend its plurality and change under its own ideal unity.

* *Confessions*, Chap. xi.

If this conception be true, we have an ontologic explanation of the "saddle-back of time" which, from this point of view, is to be conceived as representing the mode of this ideal comprehension and the extent to which it has been developed in the human soul. The *mode* is ideal and original, but the *extent* is a function of experience and seems to progress in a direct ratio to the growing wealth of man's consciousness. To the child the grasp is small compared with that of the adult man; to the adult savage it is small compared with that of the adult civilized man; to the adult civilized rustic it is small compared with the comprehension of a Plato or a Newton. The "specious present" simply measures the triumph of individuality over plurality and change; it is the resultant in the psychic sphere of the perpetual struggle of man's ideal self to overcome the relative formlessness of the actual and bring it into harmony with its own law. And in proportion as man succeeds in the struggle, the flight of the temporal becomes more rapid, its riches are emptied more and more lavishly into the basket of the present, and the circle of his individuality becoming more and more comprehensive, he feels the shackles which have bound him as a thrall to the mere temporal and evanescent, loosening their grasp, and his conscious life taking on more and more the image of the eternal.

One of the profoundest of recent thinkers[*] has

---

[*] S. H. Hodgson : *Time and Space*.

an intuition of the ontologic character of space and time, which, with matter in the form of psychic feeling, he represents as the constituents of all knowable being, and his subtle analytic is tasked in order to show how the constituents may be conceived as complicating into all forms of organized existence. But they are represented as ultimates floating at large in a universe without any absolute moorings, and when the question of absolute being comes up, as it must to all speculative minds, this thinker can discover no exit from the sphere of relativity, and finds himself confronted with the hopeless problem of developing a rational theory of relative nature out of purely relative data. Time and space and matter are ontological elements of relative being. But they are not self-explanatory. They only suggest the problem to be solved, and the principle of the solution can be discovered only by looking beyond these relative forms to the absolute springs from which they have emerged.

V

COSMIC NATURE

Hitherto we seem to have been dealing with the fragments of a world-idea. Now the whole vision begins to dawn, and in this chapter we shall seek to trace its outlines. The vision presents itself as the whole idea of cosmic nature, of the world as a sphere of mechanical activities. And just as in the former chapters we achieved the ideas of matter, space, and time, by applying the law of inversion to the outgo of the creative activities into the sphere of non-being, so here we must apply the same principle in order to reach a conception of the whole mechanical sphere.

If we make a synthesis of space, and time, and matter, we have a concept of a sphere of mechanical forces and energies, and if we realize the connection of this sphere with its absolute ground, we have the concept of a world-spirit as the transcendent ground of the world manifesting itself immanently in the mechanical categories of the world-activities. Now, the inner material principle of this sphere of world-activity, as we have seen, is causality. How then is this principle to be conceived? We have seen that it is the inner nerve of that world-series of which time is the form. But what we seek here is to determine the mode of that activity which we call mechanical causation. And in order to reach that determination, we must seek the rationale of the modification which self-activity suffers in the external sphere. Self-activity, as we know, moves ever in a circle of return upon self. It is, therefore, self-dependant and self-conserving. The outgo of self-activity into the negative sphere simply breaks this circle and translates it into a series, and the *nexus* which holds all moments in the grasp of self-dependence is straightened out, so to speak, and becomes a link of dependence upon an antecedent in time.

Causality is the activity in which this dependence on antecedents is realized. It has a double aspect. In the first place, it is a principle of external dependence. If the link of self-return be broken, then the pulsations of activity will be ever going out from their source in an external succession. Each will go out from and separate itself from each. In this aspect, mechanical causation is a self-alienating, disparate activity, which is ever breaking up unity into isolated moments and parts. But causality has another aspect equally essential, but not so overt and explicit. It is not strictly accurate to say that the movement of self-return is broken by the outgo of creative activity into the negative sphere. It is not broken, but is rather translated into implicit potency. In this form it enters the world-series as a principle of *inner continuity*. Let us endeavor to construe this. We say that *a* is the cause of *b*, and that involves the distinction and separation of *b* from *a* in the series; *b* must be out of *a* in order to be the effect of *a*. But if *b* be simply *out of a*, it is cut off from *a*'s influence and cannot be its effect; *b* must also be *in a* in order to be produced by it. In other words, there must be *continuity* as well as distinction, and the outer procession of the effect must be conceived as being grounded in an inner procession of cause.

Modern science is founded on this intuition of the dual nature of causation. It sees that the world-series and the principle of the external mechanical dependence of the parts of this series, can be rationalized only by conceiving as implied in it a continuity of the generative activity by which the series is produced. The basal insight of science thus opens to it the grounds and, at the same time, the limits of its own proper categories and principles.

Custom sanctions the employment of causation as a regressive principle for the connection of consequents with their antecedent grounds. The look of causation is, therefore, backward, and its presupposition is always, the present of the world which it seeks to ground in antecedent conditions that have lapsed. But this regressive employment of causation is merely a convention of science, and it is just as open to a progressive use. It then becomes a principle of forward world-development and evolution.

The question then arises, how is world-development or evolution to be conceived? If we reflect on the world-series we will be led, in accordance with the previously developed view, to regard it as the realization of a modified form of creative self-activity. How this modification arises and the nature of it, we have already considered. The fact to be emphasized here is that the life of the series depends on its connection with this activity, and that it can be conceived as possessing any degree of relative independence and self-sufficiency, only when the creative springs are included in it. But the inclusion of the creative springs *in* the series binds it fast to the absolute ground, since it involves the presupposition of the creative activity of the Absolute as the immanent source of the world's energy and movement. Now, if we include this creative activity in our idea of the world-series, we are enabled to reach the conception of a forward world-movement in which each antecedent section of the world will be regarded as the matrix or spring of production for each section that follows, and in which, therefore, the principle of continuous development reigns supreme.

From this point of view we see that the category of world-development or evolution is vital to the life of science. For science is the intuition of the world-series under the category of causation, and while causation says that every part of the series must have an antecedent condition, its deeper voice says also that in order to be completely explanatory, this condition must also include in it the creative ground of its being. The idea of world-development or evolution rests on this deep intuition and embodies, therefore, the ideal which science places before her, just in proportion as her intelligence rises out of the mistiness of abstractions into the light of conceptions that are concrete and adequate.

The presupposition of evolution is that in the world-series, at any conceivable point, will be found the explanatory conditions of what follows. This presupposition is valid, as we have seen, only when in the world-series, at any given point, we include the creative activity out of which the series springs. But it is not obligatory on science, in its ordinary procedure, to make a constitutive use of this presupposition. Whether dealing with nature or humanity, science may treat the presupposition as latent, and may construct her explanations in view of conditions which appear in the series. And this procedure is rendered not only possible, but rational, by the fact that the creative energy manifests itself immanently *in* the world-series, and thus translates all its realized activity into the forces and agencies of the series itself. The biologist may, therefore, determine the life-series in view of natural, mechanical causes, and the student of man may find in the nature of humanity the data of historic science. Each becomes a charlatan only when he grows negatively dogmatic and attempts to eliminate from his problem the latent assumption of the creative ground on which the rationale of evolution depends. But in science as in religion, it is not as a rule he who keeps noisily crying Lord, Lord, that enters the kingdom, but rather he who, having caught a vision of the Creator in his works, follows in a reverent spirit those mechanical footsteps which symbolize the "hidings of his power."

How, then, are we to construe the world-series when conceived under the category of evolution? The starting-point of the regressive use of causation is the present state of the world. But when science adopts the category of evolution she must transport herself back to the beginning of the series, and look forward to the present as its goal. Regressive causation is analytic, resolving the present into its past conditions. Progressive evolution is synthetic, constructing from the conditions of the past the vision of the future. And in order that it may be really explanatory the evolution process must be represented as beginning with a datum that requires no antecedent for its own explanation. This datum has been represented under the category of absolute simplicity and identified with a point in the world-series, from which all distinction and determination have been eliminated. Thus Herbert Spencer postulates a condition of absolute homogeneity as the first datum of evolution, and the process of development consists in the rise and progressive complication of distinction and integration in this undifferentiated medium. Such a conception of the world-process is open to a criticism similar to that which has already been made on Hegel's "Logic." It starts with the thinnest of abstractions and professes to show how, by a species of nature-dialectic, the world passes from category to category in the pathway of concretion and complication, until it reaches as its goal, the world with all its present riches. But as in Hegel's "Logic," it is the rich spirit of the reflector himself that supplies the motive and stages of the dialectic, so here we must seek, not in the undifferentiated homogeneous, but rather in the highly organized and developed intelligence of the Spencerian thinker, for the motives and categories of the process he describes.

We must do this unless we are prepared to admit that, either implicit in the homogeneous or transcending it, there must be assumed as a necessary datum of the process, an activity which contains categories similar to those we have read into the process. In other words, the alternatives open to us are either a subjective and psychological construction of the evolution-process which reduces the world to an ontologic illusion, or an objective ontologic construction which seeks the rationale of the world-process in its connection with the creative springs.

It is only this ontologic conception of evolution that is completely borne out by the investigations of science. Before the principle of evolution could be more than vaguely apprehended, science had to establish her great generalizations known as the laws of the conservation of energy and the correlation and transformation of forces. The law of conservation asserts that, given a certain quantum of energy, that quantum will remain constant, subject to neither increase nor diminution by the processes of nature. The empirical proof of this consists in the discovery that when energy disappears its equivalent is always found to reappear in some other form. This, however, is no complete demonstration, and cannot account for the assurance of science, which rests primarily on its refusal to believe in the possibility of annihilation. The law of correlation and transformation contains the same intuition, but it also involves an additional postulate, that of the continuity of nature through all its stages and processes. The changes of nature, therefore, including the apparent superinduction of new spheres of being and new species of force and energy, can be conceived only as transformations of forces that already exist. Science speaks with absolute assurance when she says that nature's continuity is unbroken, and that evolution can effect transformations, but is unable to create any new species or increment of force.

What is this but a deep intuition of a necessity that appears also from other points of view; namely, of the fact that evolution can be rationalized only by a presupposition that connects its process from the beginning with an inexhaustible reservoir of creative activity? Evolution is absolutely shut up to given forces. She can create none, destroy none. She can only work transformations in the materials put into her hands. She can have no voice as to how the forces she employs shall originate, nor how their existence shall be conditioned.

The vision of evolution is limited absolutely to her own things ; of the things of the creative energy she sees not so much as a glimmer in the dark. Beyond the limits of her vision rest the whole problem of the origination of natural force and the mode of its introduction into nature, the question of its possible increase or diminution in the primal springs, the whole question of the possible teleologic meaning of nature, and the relation it may bear to larger and correlated spheres of being. These problems are only for an intelligence which is able to comprehend evolution as an element in a larger system of reality.

No philosophy is complete, however, that overlooks the negative side of the world-problem. We have seen how non-being determines that modification of the world-categories which distinguishes them from absolute spiritual activities. Thus arise the relative and imperfect forms and categories of the world-series and the laws under which it proceeds. We may say that in the positive world-process, so far as unfolded, negation is held in solution but not suppressed. And that this is true will be apparent when we consider that the categories of evolution have their correlative negative categories which are inseparable from them. Dissolution, decay, and death are as real features of the world as evolution, growth, and life, and although, as will be seen in the chapter on Organic Nature, these are subsidized in a measure by the processes of higher organization, yet this result is accomplished only by a new stride on the part of the positive constructive forces of nature. The negative tendencies are only overcome and held in check, and that modern intuition which gives us the clearest vision of the processes and laws of evolution, also gives the clearest presentation of the dissolutive process. Evolution and dissolution, growth and decay, are inseparable, though antithetic categories. In the very heart of the developing process science discerns the seeds of decay in a tendency toward an equilibrium of forces, the principle of differentiation, which is a negative condition of life in a growing organism, becoming a minister of death to an organism in which the force of integration has ceased to dominate. Chaos thus confronts nature, dissolution confronts evolution, death confronts life, as an omnipresent issue. Everywhere in nature, as in the sphere of humanity, progress is achieved only through a struggle of organizing forces to overcome and neutralize negative tendencies, and the catastrophe threatened by the equilibrium of forces can be averted only by the infusion of a new increment of organizing energy and the transformation of the stagnant mass into the conditions of a new development.

We are ready now to perform the final synthesis through which an adequate conception of cosmic nature may be achieved. The ground of the world is both transcendent and immanent. Its transcendent ground is that primal energy which, as we saw, must be presupposed as the root and spring of all derivative being. On grounds which need not be restated here, we are led to posit the outgo of this primal self-activity into the sphere of non-being, where, in accordance with the law of external self-expression, it is translated into the world-energy. The immanent ground of the world is this spring of world-energy or potence which we may call the world-spirit, and which constitutes the unfailing spring out of which its forces and movements emerge. This immanent ground is related to the transcendent ground as potence to actuality, so that the ultimate rationale of the world must be sought in the transcendent activity of the Absolute.

Out of the immanent ground of the world arise the forces and categories of the world-series. We have seen how the material force which functions in cosmic nature must be conceived as dual in order that it may be relatively self-maintaining. The rationale of this duality may be found in the same characteristics which determine the series, namely, the struggle of immanent and implicit unity to overcome explicit difference and dividuality. This dual opposition is conceived as constituting in the atomic elements, to which science reduces the material constitution of things, a balance of forces which conditions the stability and continuity of the world. The immanent ground of the world is also the immediate source of the order in which the categories of development make their appearance. The primal category is self-activity. But in the sphere of non-being this is inverted and translated into potence.

The order in which this potence is translated again into actuality will be an inversion of the primal activity. Its first manifestation will be at the bottom of the scale, as far from self-activity as possible. Instead of self-activity it will be, explicitly, activity that is ever determined by the other than self. Such activity we call, in substance, material force, and in form, mechanical.

Cosmic nature is the sphere of material force acting under the mechanical form. Its proximate spring is the potential world-spirit, which actualizes itself in the world-series and in the forces and categories of mechanical evolution. The first stage of world-activity is that sphere of energies which arises from a synthesis of space and time and matter. We call it the inorganic because here mechanism reigns supreme. The unitary and individualizing force of the world is still implicit and, in a sense, transcendent, acting as a restraint on the externalizing forces, but not entering as a determinative factor into the constitution of things. In this sphere the world-series is mechanical, each part being conditioned and determined by its other. The inner law of this series is causation in its mechanical form, and the principle of its progress is mechanical evolution, the forward march of differentiation and integration in the course of which the simple homogeneity is transformed into rich and varied heterogeneity.

But it has already been made apparent that the whole sphere of mechanical development, if abstracted from its ground, becomes irrational. It can be grounded and the world rationalized only by connecting the whole world-series with the creative fountains out of which it arises, and this leads us, as we have seen, back to the immanent power that is the immediate source of the world-energies, and through this to the transcendent source of all things, the self-active energy of Absolute Being.

VI

ORGANIC NATURE

In the preceding chapters we have achieved what may be called a deduction of the idea of a world-spirit or spiritual potentiality as the immediate and immanent ground of the world's being and development. This idea of an immanent world-ground depends, as we have seen, on the postulate of a transcendent and absolute self-active spirit whose energy goes out into and operates upon a sphere of negation and non-being, by which it is translated into the inner potentiality of the relative and dependent world.

The postulate of this potential world-spirit not only grounds the series, but also the order of its development. We have seen how the mechanical categories of the cosmic sphere arise as the first *entelechies* of this potential ground. In these, distinction and difference become overt and active, determining the mechanical series and its laws, while the unitary individualizing force remains implicit and latent as a regulative and conditioning principle. But it is the law of potency to gradually pass into actuality, and from the idea of the world-spirit, already achieved, we would be led to anticipate that the next stage in the development after the purely mechanical, would be one in which the latent unitary and individualizing force of the world-ground begins to manifest itself in the series as an active constitutive principle. In other words, we would expect to see a transformation of the form of the series, and the manifestation of a force that produces individual wholes, which will comprehend and unify distinctions and parts. Thus would arise Life or organic nature.

What life is, is a question that has puzzled both science and philosophy. The tendency of science is to regard it as a complex product of mechanical forces, but how mechanism can produce an individual organism remains a mystery. Definitions of life are, as a rule, mere descriptions of its external phenomena. The physicist characterizes a living organism as a machine for generating heat and doing work; the chemist, as a body composed of highly unstable compounds; the biologist, as a plexus of organs and tissues which are adapted to the performance of certain functions, or, if he be speculatively inclined, as an inner correspondence to an outer environment. Such definitions, though true and perhaps adequate to their purpose, do not reach the heart of the subject, and fail to give any rational insight into the nature of life or its relation to other departments of nature.

The cosmic series is coextensive with time, for, as we have seen, time and the cosmic series originate together out of a common ground. But life is not co-extensive with time. Life originates *in* time, and it may also cease to exist in time. The origin of life thus presupposes a section of the world-series from which vital phenomena were absent, and in which, therefore, only mechanical forces energized. At some point in the series a new phenomenon, which we call life, originates, and this new-comer has no other antecedent conditions among the active forces of the series than the material and mechanical.

Nature presents, not a straightforward progress on a plane, but rather a hierarchy of graduated steps in an upward progress from plane to plane. Let us develop this conception a little farther. Joseph Leconte arranges this upward progress into four planes: 1, Elements; 2, Chemical Compounds; 3, Vegetables; 4, Animals; also into the four planes of corresponding force, Physical force, Chemical force, Vitality, and Will.* We thus reach the conception of the world-series as passing through three distinctive stages in its upward career; namely, those of mechanical, vital, and spiritual force, and their manifestations.

Now, naturalistic evolution is a theory which denies the necessity of grounding nature in a potential spiritual principle, and which, therefore, seeks in the mechanical antecedents of life the conditions of its genesis and development. More than this, being committed to the postulate of material and mechanical force as primordial, it is incumbent on the theory

* *Conservation of Energy.* Int. Sc. Series, p. 104.

to maintain that all other forces, vital and spiritual, are mere modifications of the material and mechanical. Naturalistic evolution has on its hands, therefore, two main problems: (1) that of the origin of the modification which is called vital force; and (2) the mechanical explanation of all vital phenomena.

In order to solve the first problem, that of the origin of life, it puts forward the hypothesis of spontaneous generation, in which the assumption is made that at some point in the world-series, when all the conditions are supposed to have been most favorable, life was generated from mechanical conditions and nature stepped into a new and higher sphere of manifestation. Now, if the fact, or even the possibility, of spontaneous generation could be established, naturalistic evolution would have some ground to stand on. But not only have all efforts failed to induce spontaneous generation under conditions which are a real test, but these experimental efforts tend toward the establishment of a negative. Not only is this the case, but the universal mode, so far as observation can extend, by which nature keeps up her organic supply, is dead against the hypothesis. If nature is capable at all of generating vital out of mechanical force, by an immediate process, this ought to be a permanent possession after life has once appeared. But, as Leconte and others have pointed out, while physical and chemical forces are being constantly transformed into vital force, an essential condition of this change is the presence of living matter. The transformation of force to a higher sphere exemplifies, here and everywhere, the law that like only produces like, and in order that a qualitative difference may arise, its analogue must be presupposed in the conditions out of which it arises.

The truth of the matter seems to be that the hypothesis of spontaneous generation involves, in addition to its other difficulties, a subtle violation of the logical principle, *Ex nihilo nihil fit*, which rationally signifies that nothing can arise as an effect or manifestation, which has not something akin to it in its conditions and grounds. In the economy of nature, life itself is one of the conditions of life. This is the law of the life-series, and it is therefore regulative of the whole sphere of biological evolution.

If we deny to naturalistic evolution its right to assert spontaneous generation, we take away from its grasp the whole sphere of origins. For in that case those transformations which an energy undergoes in passing from one sphere of force to another would necessarily be conceived as being mediated in some way by the higher force into which it is transformed. And this would clearly mark the limit of the principle of naturalistic evolution. Given any species of force, this may differentiate and distribute itself indefinitely, and thus give rise to a movement of development on its own plane. But it is strictly limited to this plane, and when the problem is, how nature is to rise to another plane and realize another species of force, here the naturalistic principle is powerless; for, as we have seen, nature only makes this step through the mediation of the higher force itself, and in order that the first step may be taken into this higher sphere, we must presuppose the archetype of the higher force as an element in the ground out of which the movement arises. And if we generalize this condition, we reach a position from which we can assert that evolution, in order to be possible without limit, must be grounded in a spiritual principle which refers ultimately back to an absolute first cause of the world; whereas, if this spiritual principle be abstracted from or denied, evolution is limited strictly to the movement of a given force along a single plane. Thus if physical and chemical force be given, the conditions of mechanical evolution in the sphere of the inorganic are present. Again, if we suppose that vital force has been somehow achieved, the conditions of biological evolution are then present. But for the genesis of these several species of force through which nature is lifted to successively higher planes of activity, the principle of naturalistic evolution supplies no adequate cause.

The second problem which naturalistic evolution has on its hands is the mechanical explanation of vital phenomena. To naturalistic evolution mechanical force, that is, physical and chemical, is the *fons et origo* out of which all other forms of force arise. Every other force must, therefore, be reducible to mechanical elements, and every form of manifestation in the world-series must be traceable ultimately to mechanical antecedents and conditions. This necessitates the supposition that life itself is a purely mechanical product; for, inasmuch as living matter is one of the conditions of the genesis of living matter, it follows, if the mythical hypothesis of spontaneous generation be given up, that the vital antecedent itself must be regarded as a form of mechanical force; for if any portion of living matter, however small and insignificant, can be successfully reduced to a pure mechanical phenomenon, the battle of naturalistic evolution has been won, and it can no longer be conceived as impossible to reach a mechanical explanation of the most complicated forms and manifestations of life.

What, then, is the obstacle in the way of the mechanical theory? It is simply this, that mechanical force cannot account for individuality. We mean by individuality here, the form of an organized product. A living organism is a body in which the mechanical forces are held in subordination to some unitary and co-ordinating principle. When liberated from the grasp of this principle, each goes its own way and the organism dissolves; but while in its grasp and under its sway, they subserve some self-centred power which controls their activities and makes them builders of the organism. The contention of the mechanical theory is that this so-called unitary and co-ordinating principle is not a principle or a non-mechanical force, but merely a product of the conjunction of mechanical forces. But this is a blind assertion which fails to realize any of the difficulties in its way. For what then is death that breaks up the conjunction? Has some mechanical agent necessary to the combination departed, or have the members of the corporation dissolved partnership by mutual consent?

The truth is that, from the standpoint of the mechanical theory, the existence of a living organism is inconceivable. Mechanical forces may develop continuous series, and they may form aggregates and compounds, but the production of self-centred individuality is beyond their province. Mechanical forces have no sense for wholes as such. They move straight forward to simple ends, or flow together into united streams. They may be equal to the complexity of an organism, but its unity, its self-centred individuality, is a phenomenon that transcends their power.

If naturalistic evolution thus fails to answer satisfactorily either of the problems that confront it, it is clear that the origin and nature of life must be dealt with according to some other principle. The weakness of naturalistic evolution as a theory of origin, arises from the fact that it cuts itself off from the spiritual principle which supplies the only rational ground of the world-movement; while its weakness as a theory of the nature of life is to be found in the necessity it is under of regarding the mechanical forces as alone primordial, and all other forms of energy as modifications of these. In view of both sources of weakness the theory plainly breaks down in its unlimited form, and must be limited in order to possess any value. We have already seen where the limitation must be applied. Naturalistic evolution cannot account for the origin of any new form of force, nor for the rise of nature from one plane of existence to another. The problem of origins must be dealt with on some other principle. Nor can naturalistic evolution give any rational conception of the nature of life. Her mechanical theory commits her to a principle of explanation which regards material forces as the only primordial forms, and seeks, therefore, to reduce all other forms to the material type. The limit of the principle of naturalistic evolution is reached when the limit of mechanical forces and laws is reached. In so far as life and organic nature transcend the scope of these, just in so far do they transcend the limits of naturalistic evolution.

The foregoing strictures on naturalistic evolution as a theory of life, are not directed against the principle of evolution. Their aim is simply to clear the ground for a more adequate conception of the idea of world-development. As indicated in the beginning of this chapter, no theory of world-evolution is adequate that does not include in it a recognition of the necessity of a world-ground out of which, as from a fountain, shall emerge its forces and phenomena. Again, no theory of world-ground is adequate that does not identify that ground with a spiritual principle. Nor is any theory of the spiritual principle adequate that does not connect it as the immanent potency of the world-development, with its transcendent source, in the spiritual self-activity of an absolute nature. The world-evolution is thus grounded immediately in an immanent spiritual potency, and mediately in the self-activity of a transcendent Creator and First Cause.

Upon this foundation we are able to conceive a world-evolution that is at the same time completely universal and completely rational. For in this spiritual ground, as we have shown, is contained not only the rationale of the existence of a relative and temporal world-series, but also the rationale of its order and the succession of its categories. From this point of view it is rationally necessary that the mechanical forces and categories in which plurality and self-exclusion are most explicit, and the forces of unitary individuality most latent and transcendent, should first emerge. The world-series is thus grounded in mechanism. But if the world be grounded in a spiritual principle, a point must come in its development when the latent and relatively transcendent force of unitary individuality will begin to show its head above the stream, a point at which it will cease to be merely regulative, therefore, and will enter into the series as a constitutive agent. Now, it is at this point that a new phenomenon will make its appearance. Just as soon as the unitary force begins to function explicitly, the nucleus of an organism will be formed, for, as though a vortical movement had been originated in some part of the series, the particles will begin to whirl and aggregate around some invisible centre, the ordinary processes of physical and chemical forces will become tributary to this new movement, and the product will be a body that is self-centred and that has within itself the principle of its own unity and conservation.

We have been representing in figure what would happen to the world-series when the spiritual force of unitary individuality begins to function in it as a constitutive agent. Dropping figure, we may say that this presupposition of a spiritual world-principle is the only basis on which a completely rational theory of organic evolution can be grounded. It places at the heart of the world a principle which, beginning with the mechanical, has in it the potentiality of a progressive evolution up to the spiritual. The continuity of the world-movement is thus secured. Not only so, but it enables us to understand rationally why there should be a movement at all, and why this movement should be upward. And lastly, it enables us to understand rationally why the progress of the world should lead it from the purely mechanical into the biological sphere.

A living organism realizes the form of individuality. It is unity overcoming and comprehending diversity. It is a synthesis, therefore, of mechanical and extra mechanical forces. On the side of its unitary individuality it transcends mechanism, and is the first overt spiritual manifestation in nature. On the side of its diversity it is a plexus of mechanical forces and processes. The mode by which a living organism develops is a species of natural dialectic, a conflict of opposite and antagonistic forces, in which the principle of unitary individuality is striving perpetually to bring the plexus of mechanical forces into subordination to itself. The life of the organism is the progressive achievement of this subordination.

But a living organism does not completely realize the essence of individuality. There is no return of the unitary force upon itself, and consequently the organism arrives at no consciousness of itself. The reason of this we conceive to rest in the fact that the unity of life is one which the spiritual principle achieves by going out of itself. It is a unity, in other words, which is superinduced upon a plexus or aggregation of mechanical elements which in themselves, that is, in their atomic constitution, remain unmodified. These elements persist, therefore, in obeying purely mechanical laws, and simply, while held in subordination to an alien force, subserve the life of the organism. When this alien force relaxes its grasp or is overcome, the mechanical elements resume their autonomy and dissolution of the organism ensues.

The achievement of the essence of individuality would involve an additional step in the spiritual evolution; namely, the completion of the circle of return upon self, and the consequent planting of a germ of spiritual self-activity in the atomic elements themselves. This would transform mechanism in its roots and ground those modified spiritual activities and categories which we shall come upon at a later stage of our inquiry. But in the stage of living organisms, this transformation has not been achieved. The unitary force asserts itself in an external manner in the aggregation and organization of unmodified mechanical elements. The life-struggle is, therefore, an unequal contest between the forces of mechanism on the one hand and an undeveloped spiritual principle on the other, in which this principle, for a time triumphant, at length succumbs to the mechanical forces, and the organism which has reached the climax of its career as a living body, starts on the downward road of dissolution and death. The continued existence and evolution of life depends not on the individual organism, which perishes, but on the biological series, which is self-perpetuating. For just as we have seen that the world is grounded by the going out of the absolute spiritual energy into potency, so we find that wherever spiritual force manifests itself as a principle of individual organization, it carries with it this constitutional power to emit its own potential in the form of a germ or norm, and thus establish the nucleus of another organism. Through this going out of self-activity into potency the biological scale is made continuous, and the basis of an evolution is secured; an evolution which depends formally on the spiritual ground-principle, and which in its process obeys those laws and categories of development and heredity which it is the business of biological science to discover and formulate.

VII

PSYCHIC NATURE

We have followed the evolution of the world-series through the stages of mechanism and life, and have seen how this progress can be rationally understood only in the light of its spiritual ground. The last and highest stage of the world-series is that of Psychic nature, in which soul becomes the protagonist of the drama. In the soul the essence of individuality is realized. We have seen how in the mechanical sphere the effect of the individualizing force of the world-ground appeared in that principle of continuity which bound the separate parts into one developing series. Individuality proper, however, transcends mechanism both in its essence and its form. In the organic series the form of individuality lifts its head above the stream and embodies itself externally in the living body. But here it achieves only a temporary and incomplete triumph over mechanism, by which its grasp is soon broken, and its continuity is secured only in a succession of perishing organisms.

The defect of individuality as it embodies itself in the life-series consists in its failure to realize a complete circle of return upon self. This, as we have seen, is the type of all complete spiritual activity, and it is the essence of individuality. Now, at the point in the world-series where this complete circle of activity is first achieved, and the world-energy is able to complete the cycle of self-return upon self, soul makes its first overt entrance into nature. Soul is that complete type of individuality which arises out of this perfected circle, and its roots are to be sought, therefore, not in any form of organism, but in the atomic sphere. The category of soul-activity is elemental, and must be conceived as arising in that sphere of primal forces which antedates all forms of organized existence.

Let us consider the modification which the appearance of this category would introduce into the world-series. If we posit the persistence of the material atoms or centres of mechanical force, then this psychic force will be conceived as arising in conjunction with the material atoms as a principle of spiritual activity. We will thus arrive at the conception of the soul as, in its elemental constitution, consisting of a duad or synthesis of material and spiritual forces; and this synthesis will be conceived as the primal centre of psychic activity.

We adopt this form of psychic dualism as a proximate conception. Its value consists partly in the constitutional basis which it provides for the recognized dualism of conscious experience,* and partly

---

* James: *Psychology*, vol. i., chaps. ix. and x.

also in the profounder view it opens as to the relation between matter and spirit in the sphere of the soul-life. This connection is so close and interpenetrating as to preclude the common idea that the soul is a pure spiritual activity that is unmodified by matter, and that it comes into contact with the material only in its organized corporeal form. Such a view reduces the psyche, in its relation to matter, to the position of a mere *deus ex machina*, capable of influencing and of being influenced only in an external and artificial way. If the common theory were the true one, then the way in which the categories of the material penetrate into the inner circle of consciousness and determine the forms of perception, would be inexplicable. No theory of the connection of the material and spiritual will be satisfactory, we think, that does not trace it to its roots in the constitution of the soul itself.

The statement of psychic dualism above given is not to be taken, however, as final. A profounder view may be achieved by reflection. Aristotle conceived the soul to be pure actuality; but he also conceived matter to be potence — δύναμις — and thus made no absolute distinction between them. He rather conceived a continuity of development from matter up to the purest activity of spirit. The view advocated here is in its main features almost identical with that of Aristotle. We conceive soul in its ideal essence to be pure entelechy, or spiritual self-activity, but in the form of its real existence it is modified by lower grades of activity. By this we mean to say that its ideal essence is not all realized in activity, but that some of it is mere potence. Now, it is the law of potence to be perpetually passing into activity, and in doing so it passes through grades, each of which has its distinctive categories and modes of action. Matter is a form of partially actualized spiritual potency, and there can be no impropriety, therefore, in conceiving it as co-existing in the same individual being with higher forms of spiritual activity.

This is the conception of soul to which we are gradually approaching. Nature in her journey upward to soul passes through the stages of mechanism and life. Now, just as the living organism comprehends the mechanism by which it is preceded, so soul is to be conceived not alone as the end of nature's evolution, but also as its epitome. Soul is a microcosm, and when we say that it is a synthesis of the material and spiritual, or that it unites in its constitution both actuality and potence, we mean to say that nature in her passage up to soul carries all her riches with her, and that in the constitution of the soul is to be found, therefore, a synthesis of the categories and activities of mechanism, life, and spirit.

Still, the conceptions of the soul as a duad, and as an epitome and synthesis of nature's evolution, are not completely satisfactory. We will only reach an adequate idea of soul by connecting it with the primal ground out of which it springs. The primal ground of the world is the self-activity of absolute Spirit. This self-activity going out into potentiality, constitutes the proximate and immanent ground of the world. Now, if we call this outgo, creation, we cannot regard it as a single act once and for all accomplished in time, for, as we have seen, time itself originates with this activity. But we must rather conceive it to be an eternal process, which has neither beginning, interruption, nor end in time. In its relation to the time-series, then, we must regard creation as a continuous process by which the world and its activities are kept in being.

In the light of this we are able to put a new construction on the idea of the soul reached above. It enables us to translate our categories of duality and synthesis into more adequate terms, and to conceive soul as a self-activity which realizes itself by passing through the lower stages represented by mechanism and life, in its progress. It will include in its unity, therefore, these moments of potency which will constitute a modification of pure self-activity and at the same time make it rationally intelligible how the activity of the soul may also include in it the lower categories of the world-series.

It also grounds the dualism of the psychic nature without making any break in its unity. The unitary individuality of the soul is its supreme category. But included in this there is a synthesis of actuality and potency. Out of this synthesis springs a dialectic which motives the progressive life of the soul. For, if we conceive the inner movement of the soul to be a ceaseless evolution of self-activity, in the course of which the moments of lower activity are passed through and both comprehended and transcended, we will be able to conceive the outer movements of experience which we come upon in empirical processes, as a dual dialectic between a spiritual principle of unitary activity and the lower material and mechanical activities, and also how out of this arises the dual form of the soul's life.

In order to realize this we have only to consider the categories which belong to the different species of activity. The mechanical, as we have seen, develop the categories of a series which is spatio-temporal in its form, while in substance, the parts are bound together into a continuous chain of conditions and consequents by the mechanical principle of causation. The spiritual activity, on the other hand, develops the closed circle of unitary individuality. Now, it is easy to see that if the soul be represented as we have represented it above, its manifested activity in experience will be a dual process. The mechanical activities will determine its life in the form of a series, each part of which will be conditioned on what precedes it in time. Thus will arise the flowing stream of which James speaks, that objective empirical self which flows along with the world-series and is held fast in the clutches of its conditions. On the other hand, the spiritual activity will be ever realizing itself in a self-centred unitary ego or self, the unitary I of the conscious life. And this unitary I, which we must regard as the form of self-activity, will be ever reaching out and comprehending in its circle the flowing stream of the objective empirical self. The process is thus dualistic, and takes the form of a struggle of the unitary self-activity of the soul to overcome and comprehend the empirical in its cycle, the result of which is that the soul-life can be adequately conceived only as a flowing temporal stream that is perpetually being taken up and transformed into unitary individuality by a principle of immanent spiritual self-activity.

By thus immanating mechanism in the soul's constitution we are able to rationally ground the dual process of its experience. Ordinarily the duality of experience is traced to the operation of the primal tendency of spirit to distinguish between subject and object. The objective empirical me of our experience is thought to be fully explained by reference to this category. But a serious difficulty confronts this view. We have seen in earlier chapters that the dialectic of absolute spirit which proceeds by means of this distinction, expresses itself in an immanent self-contained movement of distinction and comprehension. To absolute spirit there can be no flowing stream in which its life will seem to be embraced, but the flowing stream will itself be completely comprehended and made inner in the movement of self-return upon self, and no dual process of experience analogous to that of the soul will arise. The idea of soul as pure self-activity is, therefore, inadequate, and we must, in order to ground its most characteristic manifestations, take into account the modification of self-activity which the presence of the Aristotelian category of potence in the form of mechanism and its categories, introduces. The ideal movements of the soul's unitary activity correspond to the movement of absolute spirit, but these are never completely actualized. The ideal spiritual self is ever striving to comprehend the objective empirical self within its completed circle. But its efforts are perpetually aborted by the resistance of the stream and its refusal to be completely individualized. The resulting movement of soul-activity never realizes the ideal, therefore, but is simply an approximation to it under the form of a dualistic struggle of the spiritual self-activity to overcome the empirical stream and bring it into subordination to its own ideal.

The relation of the soul-activity to that of life is to be somewhat differently conceived. There is a sense in which the elemental forces of the world may be included under two categories, mechanical and spiritual. These embody the two relatively opposing tendencies toward self-exclusion and the serial form of activity, and self-inclusion or the activity of unitary individuality. The activity of life is simply a form of the latter. It represents the first attempt of nature to qualify mechanism by the principle of individuality. Now, the self-activity of spirit, as it manifests itself in soul, is simply a more complete expression of the individualizing force. There can be no dualism, then, between the activity of life and that of the soul. The soul represents a higher and more potent embodiment of that spiritual energy which is also embodied in life. The soul thus, in one point of view comprehends the life-energy in its own activity, while in another sense it presupposes it as its own condition. It is necessary in the order of evolution that living organisms should appear, and that they should reach their climax of development before soul can emerge. And inasmuch as life, apart from the mechanical forces and elements which it subordinates, can be conceived only as an individualizing function of an immanent spiritual principle, it is clear that soul is only a more advanced and perfect function of this same principle. Soul, then, in so far as it is a later comer in the world-series than life, must depend on the living organism as a necessary condition of its birth and development. But in so far as it is a higher embodiment of the same spiritual force, it will comprehend life within itself, and will therefore become the living principle in any organism in which it emerges.

Soul is thus a higher manifestation of life. It is life which completes its own circle and returns upon itself. It is, therefore, identical with the activity of spirit. It becomes the indwelling unitary principle in the organism by which it is transformed into a true individual. We do not conceive, then, that there are two principles of unity in a living organism that also possesses soul; but we conceive that the living principle has developed into soul and thus realized a higher form of life. There may be, and doubtless are, living organisms without souls. We can scarcely think that the life of an oak or a tulip is worthy of being dignified with the name of soul.

But we can see no reason to think otherwise than that the ground of that unitary force which determines the individual existence of the oak or tulip, is the same spiritual principle or potency that manifests itself also in the energy we call soul. The unitary life-principle, wherever it manifests itself, and in its lowest as well as its highest forms, is a forerunner of soul, and contains in it the promise and potency of soul-life. We do not identify life and soul, therefore, but we conceive soul to be a species of life, the highest form that it is capable of achieving in a relative and imperfect sphere.

How then shall we conceive the stages and development of soul-life? Soul originates in an organism, and belongs, therefore, to the biological scale. We may represent it, with Aristotle, as passing through the stages of vegetable, animal, and human. The lowest form of biological individuality is represented in the life of the plant. Here the organism is wholly unconscious of the unitary force that is working in it, and the life-principle may be regarded as transcendent and super-imposed on the mechanical forces and elements. In the animal the unitary principle becomes more immanent. The organism begins to feel its unity in an organ we call sensation, and upon this self-feeling the mental life of the animal grows up. But in the animal soul the circle of individuality is not fully achieved. Although the animal lifts its head above the natural stream in the function of self-feeling, yet it is not able to achieve its complete selfhood through self-distinction from the stream. According to the figure of the ancient thinker, it is half out of the slime and half imprisoned in it. The complete deliverance of the psyche is effected only in man, through an additional function; namely, that of self-conception or ideation. True psychic individuality is achieved when in addition to the feeling of self which the animal has, the soul ideates itself and distinguishes itself from the stream in which it has hitherto been merged. In man, therefore, the circle of spiritual self-activity is first completed, and a true soul having the basis of a rational and ideal life, begins to exist.

Now, as the history of the soul is thus bound up in the history of the biological series, it is reasonable to suppose that the laws of biological evolution will also be laws of psychic evolution. We have seen that, apart from its spiritual ground, life is inconceivable, and that its development must therefore rest directly on the presupposition of the spiritual ground. The same qualification applies to the question of psychic evolution. That the soul could be evolved, as naturalistic evolution supposes it to have been evolved, out of mechanical and unspiritualistic conditions, is unthinkable. Soul is a realization of spiritual potency, and cannot be conceived as having any other ground. Admitting this presupposition, however, there can be no adequate grounds for excepting the soul from the conditions and laws of biological evolution in general. We have seen how the soul is to be conceived as coming into being at the end of a series of progressive manifestations of the life-principle, including the vegetable and animal kingdoms, and culminating in the man. This is not to say that the soul of the animal develops out of that of the vegetable, and the soul of man out of that of the animal; but rather that, presupposing a spiritual principle as the ground of the world, the life-principle in the vegetable, and the souls of animals and man, may be regarded as its successive and progressive manifestations. The progress will thus manifest the phenomenon of continuous development.

The rise of the psyche will, therefore, be connected with the processes, and conditioned by the laws, of biological evolution. It may also be connected, we think, with the biological modes of propagation and inheritance. We have represented self-propagation as primarily a spiritual function, although it may require corporeal organs for its realization. The living principle in an organism projects its self-potential or germ as the nucleus of another organism of the same species, and thus the succession is maintained. There is no valid reason for supposing that, when the form of the life-principle which we call soul appears, this function will not continue. Rather we may suppose that the soul has the power to project its self-potential or germ, and that thus the succession of psychic individualities is maintained. The germ of the new organism will contain in it, therefore, the potency of the new soul that arises in connection with it, and psyche will thus be connected with psyche as closely as organism with organism.

And the soul will thus come under the biological laws of inheritance. Whatever be the true theory of heredity, souls will transmit their essential characteristics to their psychic successors, and in the transmission of spiritual as well as corporeal character a solid foundation for race experience and race destiny will be laid.

If it be objected to this view that it identifies soul too much with the phenomenal series, and makes it too completely a creature of evolution, the answer is that this is an aspect of soul-life to which full justice must be done. But in connection with the theory, the presuppositions on which it is founded must be taken into account. One of these presuppositions is, that no theory of evolution can be rational that does not trace the developing world-series to a spiritual principle as its immanent ground. The theory of naturalistic evolution is thus ruled out of court. Another and deeper presupposition is, that the immanent spiritual world-ground itself depends directly on a transcendent energy, the creative activity of an absolute spiritual Being. If we distinguish, as above indicated, between the historical conditions out of which anything arises and its ontological grounds, which supply the immediate basis of its existence, we will be able to see how the historic proposition that the soul belongs to an evolving series, and the ontological proposition that the soul is the creature of a transcendent creative Spirit, may co-exist as mutually complementary truths.

The idea of the psychic nature which we have unfolded in this chapter gives rise to several important considerations. One of these has a pedagogical interest. A science of pedagogy, in order to be adequate, must have two ideas as its basis ; namely, first, the idea of self-activity as the central category of the soul's life, and, secondly, the idea of a development of the soul's activities and powers. The first idea conceives the soul as actuality, the second as potence. Now, there is needed, in order that pedagogy may become a real science, such a conception of the soul as will make a rational synthesis of the categories of self-activity and development possible. This need we conceive to be supplied by the theory of the soul's constitution unfolded above, and by the conception of the dualistic nature of experience which it was shown to rationally ground. In the light of this theory, it is made clear that the process of soul-experience is a perpetual struggle of a thinking principle of spiritual individuality to overcome and transform an empirical nature that is dominated by mechanical categories and laws. It also becomes intelligible, that this process should give rise to an evolution of the soul's powers which follows the order of the development of actuality out of potence. This order, as the process of nature indicates, is from mechanism up to spirit. The stages of mental and moral growth will correspond in a rough way to the stages of the natural evolution, and both the intellectual and moral life will be dominated by corresponding categories. Thus in the sphere of moral growth, which is fundamentally the development of freedom, the child will be dominated at first by pure mechanical impulses, which determine its actions as the mechanical forces determine the movements of nature. At a later stage, the mechanical impulses will be organized under some external unitary principle, like that of authority. The command or wish of the parent or teacher will be the law which will introduce unity into the child's life. Later still, conscience, which is a principle of internal unity, will emerge, and with the appearence of this principle the child will begin to acquire a free standing-ground of its own as a self-determining and, therefore, responsible personal agent. With the emergence of conscience the plane of free moral self-activity is achieved, and the subsequent education of the child will conserve the development of this principle out of potence into realized free self-activity.

Generalizing the above illustration, we may say that all education is, teleologically, a spiritual function, and must have as its end the awakening and development of the free self-activity of the human spirit. This free self-activity exists largely at first in a state of potency, and must be developed by a process which will lead it from the mechanical up to the spiritual. In the stage of mechanism the life will be governed by corresponding categories. At first isolated facts will dominate the budding consciousness, and these will be related in the most naïve fashion to their most obvious and customary antecedents in time. The conceptions of the child will be passively determined by a species of natural photography, and its whole mental activity will be largely a reflex of the nature that environs it. But through the mechanical discipline of this period the spiritual potence is gradually struggling into activity. The next important step in its development will be the emergency of a category that will enable it to lift itself partially out of the stream in which it has been engulfed and to impose upon it a principle of quasi-individuality. This category is that of causation, which constitutes the inner bond of the series, and thus functions in the mechanical sphere as a latent individualizing function, binding the parts each to each in a developing chain. Causation begins to dominate the growing intelligence of the child as a rational norm, which develops in it the historical consciousness and sends it out in a perpetual search for the efficient and final antecedents of things. In this stage the passive, recipient spirit is subordinated to that of an intellectual curiosity, which cannot rest in the presentations of its experience, but prompts the child everlastingly to look inquiringly behind the presentation for the conditions that brought it forth. This period of naïve rationality, in which the budding spirit begins to assert itself, leads us perhaps to the end of the period of primary education.

The great epoch in moral development, as we saw, is that in which conscience lifts its head above the conscious stream. In the general evolution of the child's intelligence there is a corresponding epoch, when the principle of reflection makes its appearance. In reflection the spirit completes the circle of its self-activity in the return upon itself. Reflection contains in it, therefore, the germ of what we may call the ontological consciousness, a consciousness that has apprehended the principle of reason in a higher form than causation. The historical consciousness seeks the serial antecedents of things, but the consciousness that has achieved the germ of ontology asks for the grounds or reasons of the series itself. In other words, it only rests satisfied when it has apprehended principles in the light of which things are self-explanatory. The world is self-explanatory if we ground it in a spiritual principle that is sufficient to rationally explain to us the existence of the world.

Now, we conceive that the ground-principle of the secondary and higher education is to be found in this category of reflective reason in which the self-active spirit first achieves a rational standing-ground of its own as a free rational and personal agent; and the great business of the secondary and higher education will, therefore, be the development of this rational principle out of potence into actuality. For it must not be forgotten that, while the end of all culture is the quickening of the spirit, its pedagogical methods and the instruments it uses must adapt themselves to the stages of an evolution. And while a common category rests at the basis of the secondary and higher education, pedagogy only becomes a science when it acts on the insight, as old as Socrates, that the germ of reflection is at first hidden in a mechanical womb, and that it must practise a maieutic art in helping it to birth and aiding it in its struggle up to the maturity of a fully realized activity.

Another consideration is that of the connection between the empirical and rational branches of psychology. We conceive that the real connection arises through the idea of the soul. It is impossible, we think, to develop a psychology without a soul. But if we distinguish, as Bosanquet has done in his great work on Logic, between generalization and explanatory theory, it is possible to allow that the work of observation and generalization of psychic phenomena may be performed without the presupposition of any particular conception of the soul's nature. The empirical psychologist may, therefore, content himself with the general postulate of some unitary subject of experience as a working hypothesis, without troubling himself further as to its nature. This attitude will not justify him, however, either in denying the soul's existence or the importance of determining, so far as possible, its nature.

But when the science passes from the stage of generalization to that of explanatory theory, this problem of the nature of the soul immediately and necessarily arises. For explanation, as distinguished from generalization, seeks the rationale of things, and this, as we have seen, can be found only in some principle the presupposition of which renders the psychic sphere self-explanatory. The whole of the preceding discussion goes to show that the only self-explanatory principle in psychology is the presupposition of a soul conceived as a norm of potential self-activity, and which stands related to the psychological sphere as the unitary and individualizing energy of conscious life and experience.

In determining this ultimate principle of explanation, psychology passes from the empirical to the rational stage. The connection thus becomes clear, and also the light which may be reflected from the conclusions of rational psychology into the empirical sphere. For we have seen already that a rational doctrine of the soul's nature gives a new insight into the real character of the processes of psychic experience, and thus supplies important data to pedagogical science; and reflection will make it equally apparent that the same fountain will supply valuable light to the generalizer of psychic phenomena.

VIII

CONSCIOUSNESS

In the preceding discussions consciousness has been used as a datum without analysis. In this chapter we shall examine the posited element in order to determine its nature and relation to being. Consciousness is an underivable element of the real. Naturalistic evolution, which stands committed to the principle of "deriving everything from something else," is obliged here to fall back on the discredited hypothesis of spontaneous generation, in order to account for the genesis of consciousness out of the unconscious. There is no conceivable ground which can produce consciousness, except one that is potentially conscious. Now, potence is an unreal abstraction if it is not connected with a prior actuality. We are thus led to ground consciousness immediately in the immanent spiritual potency of the world, and mediately and ultimately in the nature of absolute being.

Consciousness has its primal seat in the activity of absolute being. That perfect self-activity which constitutes the spiritual essence of the Absolute must be conceived as a self-conscious activity.

This necessity will arise from one of two alternative grounds: Either self-conscious activity and the self-activity of the Absolute are to be identified, or the former is to be regarded as necessarily implied in the latter. We are unable to realize the second alternative, while recognizing its possibility. The former is not only conceivable, but also demonstrable, as we have shown in a former chapter; the form of self-consciousness and self-activity is the same, a self-return upon self. Their substance is also the same; namely, pure self-activity. Why then should they not be identified, and why should we not say that absolute being and absolute self-conscious activity are one and the same?

Josiah Royce finds in absolute Thought the point of identity between being and consciousness, and this Thought he names logos. With this mode of conception, provided logos be used to construe the thought, we shall have no quarrel. That thought is the logical prius of every other form of spiritual activity, follows by necessity from the logos conception of the self-active spirit. As we shall show more at length in subsequent discussions, the dialectic which constitutes the inner life and movement of spiritual activity rests on a dual intuition which is a function of intellection. The absolute spirit must think itself and its opposite, in order that the motives of the generative and unifying energies of creation may be aroused. The danger in the representation of the Absolute as thought is that intellection will be allowed to swallow up every other spiritual function; whereas the activities we call will and love, while presupposing thought as their logical *prius*, are not derivative from thought. We must rather suppose a synthesis of thought and will in the absolute volition, and a further synthesis of thought, will, and emotion in the absolute love.

To return, then, to the main line of reflection, we conceive it necessary to regard self-conscious activity and the self-activity of absolute being as identical. Spirit in its actuality will, therefore, always be self-conscious, and it will be the nature of a spiritual force, wherever it manifests itself, to become conscious also. Now, if we conceive the self-activity of the Absolute to be essentially self-conscious, it will be necessary, in accordance with the principle developed in the second chapter, to conceive that the same outgo of this energy into non-being which transforms it into spiritual potency, will also change its consciousness into potentiality. The immanent world-ground, while not actively conscious, therefore, will contain in it the potentiality of conscious self-activity.

The progress of the spiritual world-principle up to the stage of realized self-activity in the soul of man, will also be a process of the evolution of consciousness. In the first stages of this evolution the consciousness in which the world-movement originates is one that wholly transcends it; namely, the consciousness of the Absolute. In the stage of pure mechanism no consciousness can be posited anywhere in the world, except as a latent potentiality in its ground-principle. And this is probably true also of the vegetable stage of organic nature; for although the plant manifests the form of unitary individuality, there is no evidence that this is not external to the plant itself, or that it has any presage, even the vaguest, of its own life. Could the negative of this be established, it would then be reasonable to suppose that consciousness in some form is coextensive with life.

So far as we know, consciousness manifests itself in the world-series, for the first time, in the animal organism. It appears here in the form of feeling without ideality, and the animal intelligence is therefore rudimentary. But up to its limit it seems to realize a type that is common to it and the intelligence of man. If the animal consciousness differs, not simply in degree, but also in kind, from the human, the rationale of the differential marks must be sought, we think, not in an original distinction of type, but in the various degrees of development of a common type. If we suppose the world to spring out of a spiritual ground-principle, and its stages to represent the development of this principle from potence into actuality, it follows that the first manifestations of consciousness will be in a rudimental form, and that more adequate manifestations of the same spiritual type will appear later on in the series. Now, this rudimental form that we call animal intelligence is a manifestation of consciousness as feeling without ideality. Such a consciousness is capable of feeling or dimly apprehending itself and its environment, but it is unable to conceive itself or the environment, and cannot, therefore, make any intellectual distinction between itself and the world-stream in which it is merged. Now, this category of feeling without ideality, or, at least, in which ideality remains latent and potential, is the one under which the evolution of animal consciousness proceeds. There are gradations of animal intelligence from a lowest stage of simplest reaction upon stimulus, up to a stage which seems to differ little from the lowest manifestations of human intelligence. That these are gradations in the scale of a feeling consciousness that has not yet achieved ideality, is rendered intelligible by analysis. Feeling in comparison with ideality is relatively passive, and the supreme principle of its development will be association. For, until a consciousness has achieved a power of reflection which is a true function of self-activity, its processes must be relatively passive and, therefore, associative.

Now, analysis has reduced the principles of association to two, namely, contiguity and similarity, the former being relatively the more passive, while the latter represents a more active form of mentality and immediately underlies the ratiocinative functions proper. James, in Chapter XXII. of his "Psychology," takes the ground, and seeks to prove it by numerous illustrations, that the point of difference between the animal mind and the human is the absence from the former of the principle of association by similarity. All cases of animal reasoning in which similarity seems to be present, are resolvable, he thinks, into cases of contiguity. It is possible that this may be true, but the distinction seems strained, and we conceive a more natural explanation of the difference to be possible. For if we recognize the existence of a rudimental form of consciousness in which ideality or the principle of reflection is yet latent, it becomes possible for us to enlarge the scope of this consciousness in another direction, and to conceive it as capable of feeling the similarities and distinctions of things as well as their mere contiguities in time and space. For example, when a dog recognizes his master's footsteps or distinguishes them among the footsteps of strangers, he may feel the similarities and differences on which his recognition depends, without intellectually apprehending them at all. And when we recognize this extension of the principle of association in animals, we may also admit a corresponding extension in the sphere of what is called the animal reason. In the light of the distinction between feeling and ideality it is possible to distinguish between two species of reasoning; namely, reasoning which ends in volition and action, and reasoning which ends in a conception or logical conclusion. The latter is always reflective, while the former is possible without reflection.

To see how this may be it is only necessary to analyze a concrete case. A showman has trained a pony to select out of a series of the first seven digits, arranged in order on separate cards, the one that represents the day of the week, say Wednesday, on which the exhibition is given. He orders the pony to go and bring him the number for Wednesday. The pony goes as commanded and placing his head by the row of figures, seems to hesitate. The showman repeats, "the number for Wednesday! bring me the number for Wednesday." Prompted by something in these words, perhaps a peculiar intonation, the pony recovers from his hesitation and picks out the right card. In order to understand the processes involved in this we must connect it with the previous course of training, in which each step in the executive process has been laboriously associated with some word, or gesture, or expression of the trainer. We have only to suppose now that the pony's consciousness has the power of associating these two series and of feeling the connection between their associated parts, in order to reach an explanation of his action. And we have only to generalize the illustration in order to see how, on the presupposition of a feeling consciousness and the associative principles of contiguity and similarity, the ratiocinations of animals are explicable without the introduction of ideality.

In man the form of consciousness is completed by the appearance of ideality. The soul of man is, as we have seen, a circle of self-activity. The completion of this circle makes the function of reflection, the return of self upon self, possible, and reflection is what we have called ideality. Man's consciousness is one that not only feels itself and its environment, but also conceives these in themselves and in their distinction. The human consciousness has the power, therefore, of distinguishing itself from the stream in which its life flows. In this power of self-conception or reflection we find the ground of that distinction between the unitary self and the empirical stream of consciousness which rests at the basis of the manifested life of man. In the human consciousness we find also the same principles of association which also function in the animal. But there lies coiled up in the human soul, however low down in the scale, this principle of ideal reflection which on the theoretic side of man's intelligence lays the foundations of a distinctive development of free intellectual activity; while on the practical side it leads to the emergence of conscience and the life of free ethical individuality. Consciousness is from the start the potency of both feeling and ideality. But in the animal stage of its manifestation feeling alone is active, while ideality must be conceived as existing only as a latent potence. The arousal of this potency into the germ of an active life marks the beginning of an intelligence that we call human.

We have represented the activity of the soul as a perpetual passage from spiritual potence to actuality. A corresponding representation of consciousness will express its truth. In the developed consciousness we find a synthesis of feeling and ideality, and this, in view of the nature of the soul of which it is the expression, can be conceived only in terms of perpetual movement as a passage from potency to actuality. We have seen that the soul is an epitome, a microcosm of the world-process through which it is realized. It leaves nothing behind, but embraces the moments of potency through which it has passed on its way to actuality, in the completed circle of its life. In like manner, consciousness epitomizes the stages of its evolution. Man is an animal with an animal organism, and his intelligence includes in it the animal intelligence, as a point which he must perpetually pass through in order to reach his own standpoint. But this animal intelligence is a stage or moment that is perpetually being overcome and subordinated, and man only reaches the plane of his own true life when he has attained to the standpoint of reflective ideality and thus become a free intellectual and moral agent.

Synthesis of the ideas of the psychic nature and of consciousness here reached, makes possible another very important advance in philosophic conceptions. A self-activity that unites in it the moments of feeling and ideality, constitutes a fountain out of which spring the intellectual, emotional, and volitional elements of man's actual experience. But the soul is to be conceived also as in a perpetual movement of self-evolution in which it is ever passing from potency to actuality. The complete actuality at which it aims is not, therefore, a present possession, but an aim that is perpetually being achieved. It is an ideal which embodies the true nature of the soul, and which is constantly pressing upon the spheres of its activity as the true law of its being. Thus arises an ideal spring of intellectual, moral, and æsthetic elements which stands for the soul's true activity, and which embodies itself in man's spiritual ideals of the True, the Good, and the Beautiful. The synthesis reached above gives us an insight into the fact that the ideal is no external and visionary element in our conscious life, but that it is immanent and internal, the true goal toward which all normal psychic activity tends.

IX

MORALITY

A metaphysic of morality cannot be developed exclusively from the idea of the human soul. It must go back of this to the primal ground out of which the soul has come. The soul is proximately the highest entelechy or actualization of the spiritual principle which constitutes the immanent ground of the world. But this immanent principle is a potence which presupposes a transcendent actuality. This actuality is the absolute self-active Spirit which energizes as the ultimate ground of all things.

The evolution of soul may be conceived as the progressive development of spiritual activity. For the soul is a self-active principle. But it is not absolute, nor is the consciousness it develops the consciousness of the Absolute. We have seen that the Absolute has its own immanent consciousness, which is that of a being who is perfect self-activity and in whom there is no undeveloped potency. There can be no development, then, in the absolute consciousness. Now the soul, though it realizes at the centre of its being the same category of self-activity, yet this process of realization is an evolution or development out of potence into actuality, in which the potence and its categories are a contained moment. Actuality in such a nature is an ideal which represents its goal, but not its permanently secured possession. The ideal of the soul is thus an absolute life. But this ideal is not realized, and in the nature of things never can be. For, as we have seen, the soul carries the moment of potentiality ever with it. Its movement is a perpetual struggle up out of the undeveloped potences, a perpetual effort to overcome and transform the activities of this lower life into the complete self-activities of the ideal. Thus arises that dualistic dialectic, which James has described in its psychological aspects, of the ideal self-activity of the human spirit to overcome the empirical self and to absorb it into its own unitary individuality. And the same dialectic becomes moral when conscience emerges and the free ethical self-activity of the ideal presses upon the empirical will, as a consciousness of the higher law which its activities are to realize.

Now, as it is in the ideal ethical activities of the soul that the norms of duty are to be sought, so it is in this same activity that the soul comes into closest relation with the absolute Spirit, its ground. The form in which the absolute Spirit realizes itself to itself, we have called logos. Now, the counterpart of this absolute logos in the psychic sphere is the ideal self which stands ever as the unattained goal of the soul's activity. We shall name this the

Psychic Logos, and shall use the term always in the same sense, as a designation for that ideal soul-activity which functions as the ever unrealized end of an infinite spiritual evolution.

It is through the psychic logos that the norms of morality are introduced into the human soul. But they have their primal springs in the nature of the Absolute. Now, from the theoretic standpoint the absolute activity may be conceived as absolute Thought. But from the ethical point of view it must rather be conceived as absolute Will. Absolute will is a free self-activity of choice to which the motives are all internal. Absolute will, therefore, always and only wills itself. Even when it goes out of itself its motive is self-realization in an outer, negative sphere. But when we say that absolute will wills itself, we mean that absolute self-activity wills itself, and therefore wills that its spiritual content shall be realized.

The content of anything is the immanent quality or character of its activity. Now, the spiritual dialectic will enable us to realize the ethical content of the absolute activity. We must remember that the Absolute is identical with completely actualized spirit, and that all the highest possibilities are realized in it. The absolute Thought, then, in thinking itself will think absolute truth, and this ethically conceived is absolute Wisdom. The absolute Will in willing itself wills absolute Good, and this ethically considered has two aspects: (1) as a norm of ethical activity it is the Right, which qualitatively conceived is Righteousness. (2) As a telos or end of ethical activity it is the Good, which qualitatively conceived is Goodness. Lastly, the absolute Love energizes as the absolute Unity, and this ethically conceived is absolute Holiness, while æsthetically it is the absolute Beauty.

As will be more clearly seen hereafter, the three modes of the activity of the absolute spirit are simply different aspects of its whole or individual life. When the Absolute thinks itself, will and love are immanent in its thought. When it wills, thought and love are immanent in its volition. Now, the form of ethical activity is will, and the absolute will is a function of the whole absolute individuality. The character of the absolute will is its immanent content, and this, as we have seen, comprises the qualities of wisdom, righteousness, goodness, and holiness. The absolute will then, in willing itself, wills perfect wisdom, righteousness, goodness, and holiness. This immanent content is essential to the conception of the absolute will. Otherwise no distinction could be made between it and a demoniac will.

But when we say that morality is intrinsic we do not mean to assert that the absolute consciousness stands in the same relation to it as does the human. A little reflection will show the fallacy of such an assertion. We have shown that the human consciousness is ethically, in a sense, divided against itself. Conscience reveals a distinction between an actual and an ideal. On the one hand the psychic logos mediates to the human consciousness the norms of absolute morality which function as ideal laws. On the other hand, the empirical self is imperfect and perhaps also depraved by evil, and its will falls short of the ideal, or perhaps goes dead against it. A dualistic dilemma thus arises out of the natural conditions of finite existence and there is war in the soul's members between the law of the flesh and the law of the spirit. The point we wish to emphasize here, however, is the fact that the law of the spirit or ideal, imposes itself on the empirical self as a transcendent obligation. It feels obliged to obey a law that is objective to and above it. Obligation and the Ought are, therefore, in this transcendent sense categories of the relative, and can have no place in the absolute nature. It is a dualistic nature, one in which an ideal law presses upon the actual, that is conscious of morality as transcendent, and has, therefore, a duty. The Absolute has no duty. His activity is the activity of free immanent moral perfection.

It is through the psychic logos that the norms of morality work themselves into the human consciousness. This does not, however, free them from the law of development. We have seen that the psychic logos itself is subject to this law. There is a point in the world-series when the spiritual principle in which it is grounded incorporates itself in a human soul. This soul is dual from the outset, and embodies a dialectic between what it is in realization and what it ideally is in the perfect self-activity which is the goal of its being. This is the ground out of which conscience emerges, and conscience reveals the struggle as a dialectic between what is and what ought to be. The psychic logos in the ethical sphere is the seat of an ideal law which functions as the standard of duty.

But the soul in its unity is a developing real, and as a moral personality it is subject to the same law. The moral consciousness is at first a germinal activity. The moral life is largely potential, but it is going on to actuality and in every stage of its evolution there is present in it this sense of a dialectic between an actual and an ideal, between what is and what ought to be. If it be asked how an ideal can be subject to the law of development, the answer is that growth is the law of a being that passes from potentiality into actuality. And when this being becomes conscious; that is, begins to realize itself to itself, the duality of its nature will be revealed to it and it will not only be conscious of what it is—a being whose self-activity is tangled up in the skein of mechanism—but it will have a consciousness of the true ideal law of its nature, that of unimpeded self-activity which in the moral sphere is self-determination, and this ideal law will press upon it as the true principle of its being, a law that it is obliged to realize. But it is not necessary for an ideal to reveal actually a perfect content in order to become a standard of duty. The moral law of conscience as it reveals itself is simply a law of trend. It is the recognition of the fact that perfection is the only true end of our being, and that a perfect law—that is, a law that commands perfection—is the only law that can command our nature with unconditional authority.

Now, it is obvious that the force of such a law may be clearly recognized, while at the same time it may not be at all clear what content of duty the law enjoins. It is in the sphere of content mainly that the principle of development applies, since man must learn through a growing experience and through many different channels, what his duty is.

If it be asked further, how this moral development takes place, we answer by pointing to the whole history of humanity. Everything that contributes to or affects human development also affects moral development. The labor of pointing out the successive stages of the evolution, the forces that are active in it, and the conditions out of which it arises, is one that cannot be undertaken here. But it is essential that the movement should be interpreted in the light of its true ontological conditions. The whole process of evolution springs out of a potential spiritual principle which has its immediate presupposition in the self-activity of absolute Spirit. This spiritual potency, in passing gradually into actuality, realizes the stages of a development from mechanism up to spirit. On the ethical side of the evolution conscience stands central, for conscience is simply the ethical form of the conscious self-activity of spirit. Conscience reveals the dualistic dialectic between the realized actual and the ideal Ought which conditions and determines the form of all moral experience. Moral evolution is a movement that presupposes this dualistic struggle and the ideal function of conscience. Without this it is nugatory, for it is only through this condition that man can become a subject of moral experience at all. It is conscience or the psychic logos as ethical will, imposing its ideal law upon the human soul as unconditionally obligatory, that supplies the inner motive of ethical evolution. And it is conscience, as containing the ideal norms of character and conduct, that supplies the teleological force of the movement. Out of the moral dialectic which arises between what man has achieved and the urgent sense of something that he ought to achieve springs the spiritual activity through which all his moral riches are acquired.

There is a sense in which the whole dialectic of moral progress may be represented as the achievement of Freedom. Morality is a function of conscience, but conscience itself is an ideal will. The law of ideal will is free self-determination. Now, we have seen how the empiric will only partially realizes this self-activity. It is in partial bondage to mechanical categories. Its life flows along in the world-stream and is subject to its law of causal antecedence. While, then, the form of empiric choice is self-determination and, therefore, formal freedom, in fact this freedom tends to lapse into a species of mechanical determinism. The empirical condition of actual choice is character, and character grows largely out of serial antecedents. Why, then, is the determinist not right when he denies freedom and asserts the choice of the will to be strictly determined?

We answer that the determinist only blunders through an inadequate conception of the conditions of his problem. The freedom he denies is a will-o'-the-wisp, and the necessity he asserts has little more substantiality. It is true that the empirical will belongs to the series in the sense that what a man has been helps to determine what he is, and that what he is is the immediate antecedent of his choice. This is involved in saying that all determination is self-determination. What the determinist insists on is the fact that the self that determines is resolvable into a chain of antecedent selves, and that each antecedent self functions in choice to determine the self that follows. The determinist imagines that this destroys freedom; and he is right if the idea of the series be an adequate representation of the moral situation. But it is not, for we must take into account the nature of the soul as a principle of spiritual self-activity, and we must *identify this self-activity with freedom.* And in connection with this we must exercise our whole insight, and realize that conscience is the organ of this self-activity in its ideal form, and that out of the moral consciousness arises the intuition of a dialectic between the actual which is caught, so to speak, in the mechanical toils of the series, and the ideal law of self-activity which is revealed and imposed in conscience. We must grasp all this in our intuition, and then we will be able to attach a meaning to freedom that will bring it into vital relations with mechanism without being submerged by it. For we may admit the main contention of determinism; namely, that the choices of the will have as their immediately determining antecedents a series of empirical selves, and this will supply one of the essential conditions of the moral problem. We have to recognize in connection with this, that the essence of freedom is self-activity, and that the inner history of the soul is an evolution of self-activity out of potentiality. And in addition to this we have to recognize that conscience is the organ of this ideal free activity, and that from the standpoint of conscience the dualistic basis of moral progress is revealed.

From these data it will become apparent that mechanism is the handmaid of freedom. For freedom as self-activity is the inner motive of the whole process. And while the process itself is to be conceived as serial and as subject, therefore, to the laws of mechanical determinism, we are able to see that the motive of the process is to be teleologically rather than mechanically conceived. The teleological standpoint of morality is that of conscience, which is the organ of ideal freedom. And the process of moral experience can only be adequately grasped when we conceive it as a dualism in which the ideal force of conscience is perpetually operating upon the empirical self, which is the immediate antecedent of choice, in order to modify it, and transform it into harmony with its own law. The realization of freedom thus stands as the telos of the whole moral drama, and moral evolution is seen to be but an aspect of the larger evolution of the human soul, an unending process in which the activity of mechanism passes into the completer and freer activity of the spirit without being thereby suppressed or destroyed.

A sense of the dualistic basis of morality constitutes the richest vein in the Kantian speculations. But Kant fails to realize fully the true character of moral dualism, not from any lack of native insight, but because he has never achieved adequate ideas of being, non-being, and the nature of the soul. While he has a profound intuition, therefore, his failure consists in weakness in the sphere of its application. Kant draws from his dualistic data an inadequate conception of the ultimate sources of morality and a defective doctrine of moral freedom. He truly conceives that the norms of morality are to be found in man's rational and spiritual nature. He, therefore, makes the ideal moral reason of the soul self-legislating, and conceives autonomy to be the only true principle of morals. So far he reasons well. But because he has made a cleft between the moral reason and the Absolute, he is forced to regard the principle which finds the ultimate springs of morality in the nature of the Absolute as heteronomous and, therefore, false. The principle of moral autonomy thus becomes abstractly humanistic and irreligious, and a chasm yawns between morality and religion which nothing can bridge over.

A more adequate conception of the Absolute and of the ideal, rational and spiritual element in man's nature would have enabled Kant to escape this fatal error, without sacrificing the principle of autonomy. Had he reached a true conception of the psychic logos and its relation to its primal ground in the absolute nature, he would have seen that the principle of autonomy is not irreligious, and that when it is thoroughly applied it will lead to the subsumption of the moral idea under the idea of religion.

Kant also erects upon his dualistic basis an inadequate doctrine of moral freedom. He truly conceives the empiric will to be subject to natural causation, though he does not clearly grasp its form as self-determination in a series; and since all actual choice and action belong to the sphere of temporal succession, he concludes that freedom has no place in a world like ours. Turning now to the sphere of the noumenon or ideal, he is able to conceive a nature which is not subject to the law of natural causation, and had he been able to fully realize this nature he would have been in possession of the data for a true doctrine. But an unfortunate breach which he has already made between the phenomenal and noumenal spheres, renders him impotent. He can never reach the intuition of spirit as real, and his sphere of noumena remains empty of reality and is filled with mere possibility. True, he finds grounds of moral necessity for postulating the reality of this sphere, but postulation is not intuition, and his postulate remains a virtual abstraction. The law of freedom which he conceives as belonging to this sphere is, therefore, of no real effect, and the whole case for morality is left virtually in the hands of natural causation.

It is evident that had Kant conceived true ideas of the Absolute and of the psychic nature of man, his fine dualistic intuition would have led him to more adequate results. He would have seen the vital connection between morality and religion, and the true idea of freedom would have been opened to him. For he would have seen clearly that the recognition of natural causation as a principle of self-determination in the empirical series is consistent with a true doctrine of freedom. Conscience would have revealed to him the real nature of freedom as an ideal self-activity of the soul, which is ever operating upon and through the empiric will toward its own self-realization. Freedom is, therefore, the inner essence of the empirical process, and the teleologic law of moral achievement, without which morality would lose all its meaning and value.

X

NON-BEING AND EVIL

The practical working out of moral experience, and especially the fortunes of the struggle of the spirit to transform the empirical will, is profoundly affected by the presence of evil in the world. Evil is a factor that has been variously treated in our modern thinking. It has been identified with being as positive principle, while good has been conceived as negative in its character, and pessimism has been the resulting theory. Again, it has been identified with non-being and non-being with relativity, and a theosophic mysticism has emerged whose ideal is the breaking of the mould of psychic existence and absorption into Nirvana. Lastly, evil has been identified with non-being, and non-being with unreality, and optimism has emerged with its denial of the reality of evil, and its blind adherence to the dogma that the actual and the ideal are one, or that whatever *is* is right.

Now, in order to treat the problem of evil with true insight, we must approach it from the standpoint of the fundamental categories, being, non-being, and becoming. For the most serious defects of theories of evil have sprung as a rule either from an oversight of some of these categories, or from a confused identification of evil with some of them. In view of this we lay down the proposition that evil cannot be truly theorized except in the light of the trinal categories of reality, and also that it cannot be identified with either being, non-being, or becoming, although it has its roots in non-being.

The typical pessimist of modern philosophy is Schopenhauer. But the roots of his pessimism are to be sought in the depths of his metaphysics. Schopenhauer denies the rationality of the world, conceiving it to be the product of the blind and unreasoning impulse of a will which strives wholly without intelligence. The reason and intelligence of the world do not spring from its ground-principle, but are an afterthought, a by-product of blindly groping instinct. The rationality and intelligibility of the world are, therefore, appearance and not reality. The only realities are unreason, caprice, chaos, and mal-adaptation. Now, the metaphysical doctrine of the blindness and irrationality of the world, when carried into the ethical sphere, becomes the ground-principle of pessimism. The Schopenhauerian pessimism does not follow logically from the identification of the world-ground with will, but rather from the disjunction of will from intelligence and the identification of will with non-intelligent instinct. Pessimism does not deny that there are reason and order in the world, but these are late comers, and they find that unreason and caprice have been beforehand with them, and have sat, as it were, as the privy councillors of the Creator. The world is conceived as springing out of an irrational and chaotic root. Its tendency to mal-adaptation, to the production of misery instead of happiness, caprice instead of reason, chaos instead of law, confusion instead of order, disease and poverty instead of health and riches, is, therefore, constitutional, chronic, and incurable.

Now, after Schopenhauer it is no longer possible to rest in the easy-going optimism of Leibnitz and the eighteenth century. Schopenhauer has opened our eyes to the fact that evil is a real and very serious factor in the world. We can no longer ignore the existence of evil or treat it as a phase of good in the making. Evil is not good in the making, but always and everywhere the opposite and foe of good. But there is a root of illusion in Schopenhauer. We have seen that the universe becomes intelligible only when we undo the disjunction of will and intelligence and conceive the first impulse of being to be intelligent and rational. This is what Schopenhauer denies, but his denial carries him too far. In order that the philosophy of Schopenhauer may be rational the intelligence of Schopenhauer himself must be rational. The world, then must in Schopenhauer have achieved a stage of rationality and order. Schopenhauer says that this is a by-product, and has no more right against the nature of things than any other epi-phenomenon. Well, if that be true, the standpoint of reason and intelligence has no more right, claim, or value than any other. It is a passing phase of existence like the rest, and why should the clay cry out against the potter? In short, the logic of Schopenhauer's position leaves no ground or motive for the impressive moral which Schopenhauer draws and which alone clothes pessimism with the dignity of a serious theory. The root of illusion in Schopenhauer is his identification of being and evil. This reduces rationality and good to negativity. If being and evil are one and good, and rationality be negative, then the irresistible and inevitable tendency of the universe is toward the generation of caprice, unreason, and chaos, and against that of reason and order. It, therefore, swallows up all standpoints, including that of Schopenhauer, and leaves no ground for any theory of things whatsoever. For a little man to sit in his study and write, and seriously believe, that caprice and unreason constitute the essence of things thus involves a self-contradiction that is little less than ludicrous.

The typical optimist of modern philosophy is Leibnitz. The roots of his optimism are to be sought in the metaphysical theory on which it rests. Leibnitz distinguishes three species of evil —metaphysical, natural, and moral. Metaphysical evil he identifies with imperfection, thus committing himself unwittingly to the contradictory position that all relativity and becoming are evil. Leibnitz did not mean this, but he falls unwittingly into the mistake because he has overlooked the real metaphysical ground of evil. Or rather, he traces it wrongly to the will of the Creator, who after revolving an infinite number of world-patterns, some of which, Leibnitz lets us think, were perfect, chose the present imperfect pattern as the best practicable scheme. Leibnitz was sharp-witted enough to see that his reference of the imperfection of the world to the option of the Creator committed him logically and ethically to a conception of evil which would deprive it of all serious reality. Otherwise the goodness of the Creator would be impugned. He therefore conceives evil in both a negative and an unreal sense, as mere defect of good, as good in the making. Leibnitz shows little signs of any intuition of the fact that evil is the opposite and foe of the good, that it is that which the good must forever suppress and annul. Identifying evil thus with the unreal, Leibnitz is utterly blind to the gravity of its nature and to the serious issues in life and destiny to which it gives rise. Like the typical optimist that he is, he confounds and even identifies the actual and the ideal. For though he is not the author of the dictum that whatever *is* is right, the spirit of his general view is in sympathy with such a sentiment. Leibnitz recognizes evil, it is true, but his recognition is a kind of lip-service, for he cannot for the life of him see that there is anything seriously wrong with the world. Evil to Leibnitz is merely a kind of a disciplinary agent, which an optimist Deity employs to train his creatures and lead them to higher stages of good.

Well, the pedagogical aspects of the question should not be overlooked. But it is a shallow view of evil that would seat it in the chair of a Divinity School as a teacher of morals. The truth of the matter is that Leibnitz has missed almost the entire philosophy of evil. It is of no avail to recognize good as positive and identical with being, and evil as negative, if we do not also conceive evil as the opposite of good, and therefore real. If evil can pass into the good, or if it is good in the making or a pedagogical condition of good merely, then it has no reality, but is an appearance, and optimism of the most roseate hue is the true theory. But the whole rationality of a philosophic theory rests primarily in its insistence on the cardinal position that real opposites cannot pass into one another, but deny and annul one another. Evil is opposed to good, and must be suppressed and annulled in order that good may be realized.

But Leibnitz lacked the philosophic basis from which an intuition of the true relation of opposites becomes possible. Leibnitz had an intuition of being, but none of non-being. We must trace the relation of opposites back into the very root of spiritual activity itself. There we will see that the primal impulse of being which leads to the intuition and conscious assertion of self, leads also by a necessary dualism to an intuition and denial of being's opposite, or non-being. We must realize how the intuition of this negative or non-being supplies the rational motive for a disjunction of the energy of being and a distinction between immanent self-realization and the outgoing energy of voluntary creation. We must realize how the outgo of creative energy into this sphere of negation, in order to annul it by the generation of forms of being, in the very necessities of the case generates only the relative and imperfect, not the absolute and perfect. We must realize that this imperfection and relativity has its root in the absence from the creature of the ground and principle of its own existence. The law of the creature is, therefore, that of dependence on other, the self-existent principle on which its own existence depends, transcending it. We must finally realize that this lack of self-existent ground and consequent dependence on other which is the very essence of generated being, is the negative ground of that differentia of the creature; namely, its *mutability*, which, as Augustine profoundly saw, is the root of the possibility of evil.

From this view it becomes evident that a distinction must be recognized between imperfection and evil. We must deny that what Leibnitz calls metaphysical evil is evil at all. No relative being can exist without imperfection. If then imperfection is evil, the relative is evil, and we are led by a short-cut from optimism to the Hindu form of pessimism. For it is the tendency of Hindu thinking to identify all true being with the Absolute, and to carry the idea of the unity of this being so far as to virtually cut off all possible participation of the relative in being. The result is that the two poles of Hindu thinking are, on the one hand an unapproachable One which is the sum of all reality, and on the other a sphere of plurality and change which is pure illusion. This is the world of relativity and becoming, which the oriental mind reduces to illusion and evil, a defective veil of *Maia* which must be penetrated in order that true being may be realized. The good consists in the soul's rifting this veil of illusion and losing itself in *Nirvana* or the absolute One.

It is a curiously ironical fact that we find one of the keenest of modern thinkers thus resting optimism upon a plank which had ages before been appropriated by one of the extremest forms of pessimism. The defect in the position, whether subsidized in the interests of pessimism or optimism, is its virtual identification of relativity and evil. This renders the conclusion inevitable that the Creator is the immediate and intentional author of evil; a thought from which the human reason shrinks, and in order to escape the issue chooses rather to bury itself in pantheism or atheism, or, if it still clings to theism, to vindicate the Creator by espousing a theory of evil which identifies it substantially with good.

The difficulty is overcome when we make a distinction between imperfection and evil. The law of a created being is development, and a developing being must be imperfect. But an imperfect being may be developing along a true curve toward the realization of its ideal end. Imperfection in such a being will be inseparable from undeveloped potence. But normally this potence will go on to realize itself, and in doing so the creature is achieving the true end of its being. There are then normal types of relative and generated being which must be conceived as good. In a system of relative being, therefore, if evil arise it must arise as something abnormal, as some kind of aberration or departure from the normal types of relativity.

We cannot, then, identify evil with any of the three categories being, non-being, or becoming. And that means that evil is not necessary as an element in any system of reality. The question then arises, what is evil? Well, when Leibnitz identified metaphysical evil with imperfection he simply mistook the contingency or the liability to evil for evil itself. We cannot do better here than fall back on the intuition of St. Augustine. The creature is imperfect, and this imperfection, which, as we saw, has its source in the non-self-existence of the creature and its dependence on other, expresses itself in "a certain mutability" through which the creature is subject to contingency. Now, it is this mutability or contingency in the creative nature that is the negative ground of its fall into evil. Mutability is not in itself evil, for a thing may be, as Augustine says, mutable and yet good. Mutability is inseparable from undeveloped potency, and the capacity for growth and development is inseparable from contingency or liability to evil.

In what sense, then, is the mutability of the relative the condition of the origin and existence of evil? We must translate mutability into tendency to non-being. The normal, that is, the good type of a relative being, is the development-type, and its law is the law of growth or progress toward the perfection of the type. But the negative of the development-type and its law of growth, is imperfection, mutability, tendency toward non-being. Now, evil, in its most general and unethical sense, arises when the tendency to non-being so far prevails over the development-type and its law as either to arrest growth and initiate the opposite process of decay and dissolution, or when the being falls from its normal path into a kind of aberration. All relativity has in it the contingency of decay or aberration, and when this contingency becomes actual, then evil has originated and become a feature of reality.

What Leibnitz calls metaphysical evil, then, is not evil but the negative potentiality of evil; that is, it is that which renders a relative creature liable to evil. Evil proper is some property or characteristic of the relative which has its root in this negative ground. All evil may be classed as two species, natural and moral. Natural evil in its principle will be departure from the normal type and law of development either as a process of decay or as aberration, and its manifestation throughout nature will be disorder, caprice, destructiveness, mal-adaptation, and in the sentient sphere, pain, disease, poverty, and death.

We can only deal intelligently with natural evil

when we distinguish between the principle of evil and its manifestations or effects. The term is popularly applied to the manifestations such as pain and disease. These are undoubtedly evils. But a philosophy of evil must emphasize the principle rather than the mere manifestations. Now, it is coming to be a recognized doctrine in the psychology of pain, for example, that it has its root in some departure from the normal type and its law, either in functional failure of the life processes, or in failure of the organism to adapt itself to its conditions. Not only does this confirm the theory of evil we are defending here, but it also indicates very clearly the teleological character of the idea of evil. Evil is departure from the good and must have its primal significance in its relation to the good. But for a developing creature good can only be teleological, and it will be expressed in the end or ideal which the law of its being is realizing. The good of a creature will thus be the whole meaning and rationale of its existence. It will include its whole positive reality. The evil of a creature will be the opposite of this, the negative of the positive content of the good, in that it tends to defeat and annul the good end. Whatever tends thus in the negative teleological direction, produces the manifestation of evil in nature and sentient existence—disorder, destructiveness, lawlessness, pain, disease, and poverty.

Moral evil arises only as a function of the will of an intelligent and personal agent. Moral evil superadds the element of choice to the generic concept of evil. Choice or option is thus the differentia of moral evil. How then shall moral evil be conceived? In the first place it is evident that evil must be chosen in order to become moral. Mere spontaneous aberration from the good can never rise to the gravity of moral evil. But the choice of evil implies an option, and this must be an option that is teleological and in view of alternatives which the dual nature of the agent places before it. This is a vital part of the theory, for if the nature of the agent were monal it could have only one constitutional good and the dilemma of choice between good and evil could not arise. The Absolute, whose nature is conceived to be monal, must also be conceived as free from temptation. The evil is that to which the absolute nature is opposed, and its choice is essentially an annulment of evil. But the psychic nature of the creature is dual, and there is a perpetual dialectic between the empirical will of the actualized or empirical self and the law of conscience or the will of the ideal self. Man's dualistic nature thus confronts him with an everlasting option between the ideal and the end to which the empirical will is drawn.

This is the cardinal moral situation out of which the whole drama of good and evil arises. Moral evil arises when the empirical will asserts itself against the ideal. It thus cuts itself off from the spring of its rationality and spirituality, and becomes the organ of capricious impulse and unspiritual and animal propensity. The negative thus gets the upper hand, and the empirical will having broken with reason and spirit, yields itself to the lawless forces of caprice and passion. The result, if the rebellion continues, has been vividly portrayed by Plato. The steeds of the lower nature having overcome their guide, take the bits in their teeth and plunge madly downward with chariot and driver toward the abyss. This figure of Plato's symbolizes the lawlessness and destructiveness of the empiric will when it has asserted itself against the ideal, and the fall into depravity and moral ruin that inevitably follows.

Again, the negative character of evil comes out clearly in its moral form. There is involved, it is true, the choice of some end which is conceived to be a good. But this does not constitute the act morally evil. It becomes moral evil only as it is a rebellion against the ideal good which is imposed on our nature as a law, and the evil arises out of the fact that we voluntarily annul and negate what we recognize at the same time we ought to choose as our true good. Our choice becomes moral evil when it repudiates the higher ideal good and falls on a lower supposed good. All moral evil is thus in its essence a rebellion against good and the taking of a negative, destructive attitude toward it.

The most aggravated form of moral evil embodies itself in the will that we call satanic. This last stage of moral obliquity is finely embodied in Milton's Satan, who although a rebel against God and fallen into perdition, has still some remains of his former glory in his nature. He does not become a complete devil until, after reflection on his defeat and fall, he deliberately renounces his allegiance to good and chooses evil; that is, rebellion and warfare against God, as his good. Here the place of the ideal good is deliberately vacated of its true occupants, righteousness, goodness, and love, and unrighteousness, wickedness, and hate are enthroned in their stead. The normal relations between good and evil are thus completely inverted, and a demoniac will holds the place of the ejected ideal. The Spirit is thus quenched, which is the unpardonable sin of a creature, and the lost soul has before it only the abyss and an everlasting downward progress in evil.

What light does this view of evil throw upon its relation to the absolute Author of the world? It is clear that we cannot affirm unqualifiedly either that the Creator is, or that he is not, the author of evil. We have seen that evil is no necessary part of the relative order. But its root, the mutability and contingency of the relative, is a necessary feature, and this has its presupposition in non-being. The Creator does not generate evil, but he generates conditions which have the contingency of evil in them. Why then is the Creator not morally responsible for evil? and how can the system of things in which the contingency of evil exists be any longer regarded as good? It is clear that moral responsibility could not be escaped if the option of creation is between a perfect and immutable, and an imperfect and mutable world, both of which are possible. If we carry the idea of absolute power to the extent of including this dual possibility in its scope, then the actual imperfection and evil of the world impugns the goodness of the Creator and leaves no distinctive basis for religion. But if the whole doctrine of being, non-being, and becoming as unfolded in this treatise be true, then the option supposed above is a fiction. The very facts that creative energy is outgoing and not immanent, and that created being must originate not immanently, but out of the Absolute, in non-being, carry with them the necessity that created being should be imperfect and mutable. Only the uncreated and self-existent Absolute can be perfect and immutable in its nature. The option then which really exists and which confronts the creative intelligence is a choice between non-being and becoming. The creative energy must forever remain quiescent in face of the intuition of the outer sphere of pure negation, or it must rouse itself volitionally to an effort to generate being where now pure negation exists. If, now, the option is between non-being and no created existence, and created existence which shall be imperfect and contain in it the contingency of evil, the moral situation is completely altered. It is better that becoming or relative and imperfect being should take the place of pure negation and non-being. The spirit can only assert itself against the negative by letting free the creative energy and generating in the sphere of its opposite its own image.

The existence of evil is, therefore, not inconsistent

with the supremacy of good. The development-type and law of a relative creature, as we have seen, is good. Now, if the contingency of evil is inseparable from this development-type and law, and if this contingency results in actual evil in a given system of relativity, it is possible for such evil to exist and be real, without thereby vitiating the constitution of things. In other words, it is possible that the evil of the world is a subordinate feature of reality, and that the force and trend of the good tends continually to annul and transcend the evil. The possibility of this will become more clear if we view the world from the teleological standpoint in the light of that world-idea which to the Absolute includes within it the whole world-process. If the world-process when comprehended under the world-idea is good, then it stands justified, notwithstanding the negative feature which has been its inseparable accompaniment. It appears then, that the final judgment of evil must be teleologic, and that its nature will be largely determined by the conception we are able to reach of the end and purpose of the world.

It is clear then that neither optimism nor pessimism supply us with an adequate theory of evil. Optimism treats it altogether too lightly, while pessimism sacrifices the good to the evil Moloch. A more adequate view than either is meliorism, which while recognizing the reality and gravity of evil, subordinates it to the good and believes, therefore, that the condition of the world is not altogether hopeless, but that improvement is possible. The meliorist, with a keen intuition of the evils that are eating into the fibres of the world and humanity, will yet not lose hope but rather find in these a motive for spiritual activity. For although the end and supreme category of things is the good, this can be attained only through perpetual struggle. We must be continually rising above and crucifying our empirical selves. This is a universal law of progress, and in its realization man will find that he must not only avail himself of his own most strenuous endeavors, but also of the power that transcends him.

XI

COMMUNAL NATURE

Lucretius pictures man in his primitive state as a naked savage dominated by animal instincts, destitute of the arts of civilized life, wandering over the earth without shelter, or finding a temporary lodging in caves, and subsisting on berries, nuts, and the uncooked flesh of animals. He represents him as anti-social, engaging in a hand-to-hand struggle with his fellows, and making war the chief business of his life. Out of this war of antagonistic interests sociality gradually emerges; fire is discovered and man becomes the cooking animal; clothing and habitations are invented, speech is developed, and man becomes the rational animal and evolves gradually the varied arts and complex organisms of civilized life.

The Lucretian model has served for a whole school of modern publicists, of whom Hobbes is the chief, who represent man as being, in a state of nature preceding the birth of social order, a purely individualistic, anti-social, and warring animal, who in pursuit of his own selfish interests is in a state of perpetual conflict with his fellow-mortals. These publicists follow Lucretius in representing the germs of sociality and civic order as springing out of these anti-social conditions, and as being, therefore, a kind of artificial and conventional growth superinduced upon a soil that is primarily alien to them.

Another school, of which Aristotle is the first and greatest exponent, takes an opposite view, representing man as by nature a political animal, containing in his nature from the start the germs of sociality and civic order. The representatives of this school do not deny an evolution of sociality and social forms. They in fact assert it as a cardinal doctrine of their creed. What they do deny is that the growth can be regarded as in any sense artificial or conventional, or that man ever existed in a state of pure antagonistic individualism. They maintain that the evolution has as its necessary presupposition a rudimental sociality, and that the social life and order which arise are normal and natural.

Now, there is, without doubt, a large measure of truth in the Lucretian view. For, aside from the question whether or not man, historically, began his career as a naked and quarrelsome savage, it must be admitted that there are forces in man's nature which antagonize the social order and which must be overcome, therefore, before the social order can be established. If we name such forces individualism, it follows that the grounding of the social order will involve a conflict with the individualistic forces, and that the development which ensues will have its inception in a condition of things in which the individualistic and antisocial forces dominate. The primal condition will thus be one that is explicitly and overtly a state of warring individualities, hostile to social organization.

What this theory overlooks or ignores, is the presence in human nature of implicit but real social instincts and forces, and this oversight blinds it to the real nature of the struggle out of which the social order arises, which is not a mere aimless and fatalistic onset of individualistic forces, but rather a duel between these and their enemy, the developing energy of social order. The deeper intuition of the school of Aristotle realizes this fact, and while admitting the warfare, is able to put a different and more rational construction upon it. Recognizing the fact that social and civic order grows out of a struggle of conflicting forces, they see in this struggle the perpetual effort of a unitary principle to overcome and transform the forces of division and disorder.

All theories rest on the common presupposition of an underlying *human* nature. Frog nature, or in fact the most gifted animal nature, would not serve as a basis for the structure that is to be erected upon it. Lucretius himself recognizes this in the fact that his naked savage dominated by animal instincts, is a very different type of animal from lions or tigers, who also have their unending warfare, but out of it do not obtain the rich result which falls to the lot of man. Lucretius and Hobbes in truth assume on the part of the human animal, a wealth of capacity which belies their contention that his rationality and civic and social life have emerged out of conditions from which their rudiments were absent. For why, under the stress of antagonism, should all this rich fruitage come if all the parties to the conflict are purely individualistic forces? The answer will be, of course, that man is a creature who is capable of learning the lessons of experience, and who, seeing that unrestricted antagonism defeats the end he has in view, therefore, calls a halt and sets up a tribunal for the regulation of his lawless tendencies.

But this answer contains the very assumption that destroys it. A creature that is capable of drawing such lessons from experience must already have the germs of rationality in its nature, and in the lull of passion it will be the still small voice of reason that will be heard speaking of a better way. If we assume that man in his original nature is a creature of purely selfish and individual passions, then we are logically committed to the conclusion that any principle of conduct which may arise out of such a soil will be selfish and individualistic also. Men will, therefore, never rise above selfish individualism. The only escape from this conclusion open to the advocate of the theory in question, is the old recourse to spontaneous generation, which, to use Hume's phrase, can produce anything out of anything. But for that very reason it is worthless.

The truth of the matter is that human nature has been slandered and that man is not a purely selfish individualist, but has in his nature a *germinating sense of justice,* which is the root-principle of altruism and social and civic order. Even social philosophers of the Aristotelian school have not always apprehended all the implications of this truth. They have contented themselves, as a rule, with pointing to the social relations as the soil out of which the social institutions have sprung. But they have overlooked the fact that the social relations presuppose something more ultimate than themselves; namely, a social nature or consciousness out of which they spring. Otherwise the organic sexual instinct would not lead to the family, nor would there proceed from this the germs of the community and the state. Underlying the question of the social relations is the more fundamental one, as to what kind of creature the bearer of such relations must be.

It is evident that social relations cannot rest on the presupposition of a nature endowed only with organic instincts and individualistic passions. To assert that it could, would be to enter the school of Hobbes by the back door. It is necessary, in order to ground solidly an adequate politico-social theory, to postulate a communal principle or force in man's nature as the basis of his social and civic development. Such a principle is found, we think, in the idea or sense of justice.

The old Greek thinkers of the Socratic school manifested not only a sound instinct but profound insight in the place they assigned to *Justice* in their politico-social speculations. Socrates regards it as fundamental and is constantly seeking its definition. Plato lays it at the foundation of his Republic as the principle of all communal life. Aristotle gives it a central place in his political theory, and defines it as a principle of equality in the distribution both of awards and possessions, and Aristotle's definition has been the basis of modern conceptions of what is equitable and right, as between man and man.

What is needed, then, is an analysis of the idea of justice as the basis of communal consciousness and life. The first step in this analysis will be found in the fact that the conception of justice as a principle of distribution is not its ultimate idea. Underlying distribution must be some criterion or standard, and this the definition includes in the term equal. Equality is then a simpler idea than Justice. Now, equal comes originally from the Greek verb εἴκω, which means primarily to be like, and then to be fitting, and then to be right, seemly, or reasonable. Justice is from *Jus*, which means primarily that which binds or constrains. In the light of its derivation, then, justice is the idea of equality with the idea of authority attached to it.

Terms swing loosely on their etymologies, but these in general indicate the kind of reflection out of which they have arisen. It is clear that the Greek root εἴκω from which equal is derived does not embody a primary reflection, but has a presupposition. To be like presupposes a standard of likeness and the progress of the reflection from likeness to fitness and reasonableness indicates what the primary presupposition is. It is simply the self when it has become conscious of itself and thus realized its own independent unitary individuality. We saw before that this is the point where that ethical consciousness arises which reveals man to himself as a free moral and responsible agent. This ethical self is the presupposition we are in search of. The reflection of εἴκω is founded on this primary reflection which reveals the self to itself as a free ethical individual.

Now, the further question presses, why this ethical self-reflection should go beyond itself and include other individuals. We strike here the root of the whole matter. If we revert to the primal category of being, that of self-activity, and translate this activity into will, the outcome will be the notion of a will that is self-willing. Now, we have seen that conscience is to be conceived as such a will. But a will that is self-willing, *by virtue of that fact transcends particularity and becomes universal.* Conscience, as we have also seen, is the principle of ethical individuality, since in it the soul rises to an assertion of its free personality. The conclusion follows that the conscious activity in which man asserts his own ethical personality, is the activity which also asserts itself as universal. True ethical personality is therefore universal.

Kant had an intuition of this truth when he deduced from his conception of the moral will that of the universal legislator whose dicta are binding on all rational beings. But he did not clearly show the connection by pointing out that moral will and universality come to light in the self-same reflection. Had he done this the relation of his moral principles to legislation would have been clearer.

Returning now to the main line of reflection, we see that equality is grounded in this self-assertion of the will of a free moral personality as universally binding. Justice adds to this idea that of the moral will as a law-giver whose commands are, therefore, universally binding in the sphere of moral personality. If now we assume that man is the bearer of such a principle as this, it will follow that when he becomes conscious of the existence of other beings, like himself, the principle of justice will assert itself as a law of *reciprocity* among these beings, and each will feel obliged, just in proportion as he arrives at a clear conception of the dignity of his own person, to recognize and respect a corresponding dignity in the persons of others.

It is only necessary to conceive a being endowed with the organic instincts and selfish passions which the Lucretians picture, as also having in his nature the germs of a principle of justice as analyzed above, call it sense or instinct or what you will, in order to see how such a being may and will naturally and normally develop a communal consciousness, and out of it the elements of social and civic order. For in the inevitable conflicts and antagonisms which the exercise of the instincts for self- and race-conservation will engender, the sense of justice will also enter as a moderating force. And since most of the conflicts will arise in connection with the share each one is to have of the goods and ills of life, justice will function as a principle of distribution. The sense, however obscure, that the personality of your antagonist is as sacred as your own will have its influence on your treatment of him, and if you have succeeded in wresting from him the whole proceeds of his day's toil, this sense will operate in your bosom as an evil conscience and will prompt you to make an equitable restitution.

Now, what we assert is that the existence of the germ of this ethical principle of justice in the nature of man is the real presupposition of the Aristotelian politico-social theory. It supplies what we have seen is the great need, a rational foundation for those social relations which the theory postulates as the basis of social evolution. And it is their oversight of this principle, or their positive denial of its necessity, that renders the opposing theories irrational at this point. In order to rationalize the picture of Lucretius and Hobbes, we must endow the naked and militant savage not alone with organic instincts and selfish passions, but also with the germs of a sense of justice. There will be hope then, that in the intervals of his heated conflicts with his fellows, the voice of reflection will be heard giving him some dim intuition of the fact that his antagonist is his neighbor, to whom he should give the same measure he would hope to have meted out to himself.

How, then, is the principle of justice to be conceived in its adequacy as the constitutive force of the communal nature? The elements of our answer have already been given. The principle of justice, when translated into its most adequate form, is simply the universal ethic will. Its norm is to be found in the individual conscience, which is the conscious will of the ethical personality in man's nature, and we have only to conceive conscience as comprehending under its unitary principle all individual centres of moral activity, in order to reach an adequate conception of the nature of justice. Justice is the voice of the universal ethic will, and as such is the immanent principle of communal activity and life.

This does not mean that sociality depends exclusively on the sense of justice among men. Men are brought together by the organic instincts, by various relations of dependence. No man can live to himself or without the help of his fellows. But all these connections are consistent with selfish individualism, and on the assumption that they are the only original endowments of man's nature, there is nothing in them to render the birth of real altruism intelligible. Altruism is not a system of relations, but rather a spirit in which relations are viewed. Why should not the sense of man's dependence on his fellows but tend to foster his selfishness and render his egoism more sensitive and exacting? Again, sympathy as well as a sense of a certain community of relations are social forces. But sympathy, wherever it is not the emotional side of justice, is a blind feeling which may co-exist with the grossest selfishness, while selfishness is apt to be blind to the community of interests, and when it does realize them, subordinates them not to any genuine ethical principle, but to maxims of prudence.

The principle of justice alone supplies the "holding turn" which is necessary to translate all the forces and relations we have noted into terms of sociality. Under the moulding influence of justice the organic instincts are modified and touched with ethical feeling, while antagonisms are softened and conflicts are mediated. In its light the solidarity of interests becomes apparent, and conflicting interests, where they remain unmediated, are arbitrated before a higher tribunal. Under its transforming touch sympathy becomes wide-eyed love and regard for human kind, while the selfish passions are more and more restrained within the bounds of moderation. Thus the foundations of social and civic organization are laid, and upon these man through his checkered experience is able to build the fabric of his communal life.

The principle of justice as the ground of communal nature is to be conceived as the communal conscience, and therefore as an ideal will. This enables us to determine the real form of the dualism that underlies the social life of man. The terms are, on the one hand, a plexus of forces which are either anti-social and disintegrating, or without ethical import. This plexus, when viewed in the abstract as unmodified by any other influences, does not tend to lift man above the level of egoism. On the other hand, the principle of justice functions as an ideal communal will, and as a norm of social organization. Man as swayed by the unethical forces is an egoist, but the ethical forces are altruistic and tend to subordinate the unethical elements of his nature to altruistic laws. If then we conceive the unethical forces as constituting an egoistic will, and the ethical as constituting an ideal altruistic will, the communal dialectic may be represented as a struggle between the egoistic and altruistic wills in which the latter makes perpetually for the social life of man. The conflict is ever waged on these lines. The egoistic will ever tending to selfish individualism, while the effort of the altruistic will is to subordinate egoism to the social and civic order. This dualism is the inner motive of social development. Subject to the modifying influence of the environment, it gives rise to existing communal organisms in any given time and place. Now, the determining force in such an organism is called *sovereign*. How then shall the sovereign power of a community be construed? We may regard the community itself as rising out of unethical grounds, and then we will be committed to the view of Hobbes; namely, that sovereignty is unethical, and therefore arbitrary. Or we may conceive the community as grounded in ethical principle, and then sovereignty will be affected by moral quality. The whole view elaborated above is consistent only with the latter supposition. We conceive the community to be an ethical individual whose sovereignty embodies itself in a communal will. Will is not arbitrary unethical force. But where there is will there is also conscience, which, as we have seen, is an ideal and universal will that imposes its law on the actual. And where there is conscience there is a consciousness of right as well as a consciousness of responsibility. We do not mean to assert that the individual conscience as such dominates or should dominate the community. But the same ethical norms are active in conscience whether it be an organ of the individual or an organ of the community. The communal will thus stands related to a communal conscience in a way that is analogous to the relation of the individual will to the individual conscience. The communal will, like that of the individual, may act capriciously and arbitrarily. But the relation of the individual will to conscience imposes upon it the ideas of right and responsibility. In like manner there is a public conscience which contains the norms of communal right and responsibility. The public conscience like the individual is an ideal will founded on the principle of justice. It arises through the sphering out of the individual conscience into an organ of the community. The communal conscience is the conscious recognition of justice as the norm of communal right. Thus the idea of Right arises in the social sphere. Communal right is simply justice, regarded as a standard or law of action, and obligation in this sphere is the pressure of this ideal standard on the will of the community.

It cannot be said, then, with truth, that the communal sovereignty is unethical, or, on the contrary, that it is the basis of ethical distinctions. It cannot be said that it creates right or justice in the ethical sense. It is an inversion of the true order to say that any thing is morally right or just because it has been ordained by law. It is legally right, of course, but that is tautology. The community that utters the law rises upon the principle of justice. This is the conscience that functions in it, that gives it the sense of right and responsibility, and that infuses all its energy with ethical quality.

The community is an ethical individual endowed with will and conscience. Like all true individuality, its life is a process which is to be construed as a dialectic struggle between an actual and an ideal. The actual is the plexus of forces and conditions which determine the actual energizing will of the community. The ideal is that sense or principle of justice which functions in the communal conscience. The progress or evolution of communal life arises from the perpetual dialectic between these forces, the communal individual uttering its will under the pressure of the communal conscience, which is ever striving to bring it into harmony with its own law. The progressive outcome is the uttered life of the community, its body of laws written and unwritten, its civil and ecclesiastical organisms, its constitutions and forms of government.

It is only when we view the community as an unfolding individual, that we can determine its true end or good. The immanent end of individual activity is self-realization. But it is self-realization in view of an ideal which imposes the standard of the self to be realized. The immanent end thus transcends the actual, and through translation into the law of the ideal becomes the ideal good and true good of the individual activity. We may apply this without modification to the community. The immanent end of the communal individual is what it is realizing in its progressive life. But the communal conscience imposes upon its activity the standard and law of ideal justice. The true end thus transcends the limits of actual self-realization, and takes the form of an ideal and teleologic good. The good of communal activity is, therefore, the realization of the ideal communal life. What, then, is this ideal communal life? The principle of justice will here be our true guide. That principle, as we saw, is one that imposes on each individual's will the obligation to regard the right and good of every other individual as equal to his own. Justice thus effects an equation of individual wills, and thereby subordinates them to a common, universal standard. The idea of the community is that of an organism in which individual wills are subordinated to the will of the whole, and the ideal community is one in whose will the principle of justice is completely triumphant.

We thus reach the idea of an organism in which justice is completely dominant, an organism in which the universal right comprehends and realizes all individual rights. And since this universal right thus conserves the true individuality of the members of the community in realizing its own highest self, it becomes the highest good of the community. For it is an ideal good of the whole in which the ideal good of all the parts is contained. The notion of such an organism is an ideal that is never completely realized. But it functions in every communal organization as its conscience, and it is the guiding light of all true political philosophy and statesmanship.

The rise of the community is a momentous step in the evolution of the free spirit of man. As the old Greeks clearly saw, it establishes the conditions in which alone man's highest and truest activities can be realized. The community is an ethical individual and has its roots in the spiritual principle which underlies the world. We have seen how this principle embodies itself in the psychic constitution of man, and lays the foundation of the evolution of free spiritual life. We see here how it achieves a further embodiment in a communal life of humanity, an embodiment whose ideal is the realization of spiritual activity in its highest and freest form. It is as an organ of the communal consciousness and as an intelligent member of a communal organism that man reaches the highest development possible to him in this world, and in losing his life in the common life of humanity finds it again in a higher and nobler form.

XII

HISTORY

The idea of communal nature mediates that of Humanity in that it supplies the sphere in which the common life of man is unfolded. The motive which leads the individual consciousness to sphere out into a universal life is practical, springing from the activity of the ideal principle of justice. When through ethic principles, however, man has achieved the basis of a common life, this gives opportunity, as we have seen, for a freer and larger exercise of his spiritual activities, and his whole rich nature pours the fruits of its energies into the common lap. The idea of humanity is that of a common life in which the potencies of individual lives are realized.

This idea may be conceived either statically or dynamically, and two branches of humanistic science will thus arise which may be styled respectively, Anthropostatic and Anthropodynamic. These will have the same content, the output of the human spirit energizing in the communal sphere; but anthropostatics will treat this output under the category of work done, as the achieved product of the psychic activities; while anthropodynamics will proceed under the category of active energy to investigate the processes in and through which the results are obtained.

The idea of anthropostatics is that of culture, a term that is used here as identical with civilization, and stands for the whole achieved product of man's activities in any great age and place. It will include Science, Art, Religion, and Social Organization. The idea of anthropodynamics is that of History. History is culture conceived in the making, and therefore under the categories of force and energy. History deals with the common life as a sphere of becoming which expresses itself in an evolving series. It treats science, art, religion, and the social organism, therefore, not as products, but under the category of development. The idea of history suggests its fundamental problems, which are, (1) the nature of the historic series, (2) the conditions of historic progress, and, (3) the laws of historic progress.

History deals with a series. The life of humanity embodies itself in a succession of manifestations. This succession is a conditional one. Not only does it represent a temporal order, but also a dynamic and causal order. If we look at it externally it presents the unbroken appearance of a flowing stream. When we penetrate deeper we discover that the stream is subject to the law of conditions, that each phase of its manifestation is traceable to its causal antecedents. And when we cast our glance forward the phenomenon presented is that of evolution. The life of humanity is a procession, a becoming, in which every stage is found to rise out of some series of conditions that precedes it.

The most obvious view that we can take of the historical movement is, therefore, a mechanical one. The categories of the cosmic series may be applied without modification to the historic series, and everything may be conceived as springing out of antecedent conditions by a species of invincible mechanical necessity. This view leads, therefore, to a kind of fatalism which eliminates freedom from the life of humanity, and with it the larger part of its ethical significance. History, from this point of view, is simply a species of statistic gathering for which a strict mathematical calculus is all that is needed in order to deduce the past and work out infallible predictions for the future.

Now, fatalism would be true if nothing had been overlooked in the inventory. But there has been an important oversight. It is true that if we cut the plexus of historic tissues transversely at any point, we will find that its strands are continuous, and this may seem to demonstrate the fatalistic conclusion. But it is forgotten or denied that what has been cut at the centre is the quivering heart of humanity itself. And this quivering heart is the self-active spirit of man himself. If we eliminate the self-active human spirit from the problem, we have left a corpse and not a living organism. If, however, we count the self-active spirit as one of the factors, then our evolution is secured, but it has lost its fatalistic aspect; for a series of manifestations which has at its heart the pulsatory movement of a self-active spirit, may in the order of its outward manifestation obey the law of mechanical necessity, but its inner spring will be a fountain of free activity.

The question here is not one of fact, but rather of interpretation. The fact is a humanistic world-series that realizes the phases of an evolution. The problem is how this evolution is to be construed? We have seen, in treating of other aspects of the world-series, that evolution is unintelligible and irrational, if we do not ground it in a spiritual principle. From this point of view, mechanism, and in particular mechanical evolution, is to be conceived as a form of energizing which presupposes, but does not contain, the self-activity of the spiritual principle. To characterize the humanistic series as mechanical, would, therefore, be to place it on a level with the cosmic series, and to affirm that while it presupposes, it does not contain, the spiritual principle.

But such a view is not tenable. We have seen how in the psychic stage of the world-evolution, the self-activity of spirit enters into the series as its central category, so that the phenomena of the psychic series are not open to purely mechanical construction. Now, the psychic series simply spheres out into the humanistic world-series, at the heart of which, therefore, functions the spiritual energy of the psychic nature. The humanistic world-series is no more open, then, to the purely mechanical construction than is the individual psychic series, for it contains in it as its central category the principle of spiritual activity. And where there is spiritual self-activity, there also is the principle of free activity. Freedom thus enters into the series, and functions at the heart of the mechanical conditions as a force which transcends mechanism and lifts the whole historic process above the plane of the purely mechanical.

In order to discover the conditions of historic progress it is necessary, first, to realize the problem to be solved. This is not purely spiritual or purely mechanical, but rather mechanico-spiritual. It is the problem of the development of a spiritual activity under mechanical categories and conditions. The elements to be taken into account will be, (1) the historic series itself, which may be analyzed into two parts, the inner activity of the spiritual principle and the form of mechanism or outer necessity which this activity assumes; (2) the external and limiting conditions of the series as a whole.

Now, the central element of the series which determines its essential character, is the spiritual energy that works at its heart. This spiritual energy we have already treated in the chapters on Psychic and Communal nature, and have reached the conception of it as a self-active principle whose movement or dialectic is to be construed as an evolution out of potentiality into actuality. It is this immanent dialectic which constitutes the inner motive of the evolution, and also determines it as spiritual in its character. But as we have seen, the order of development in a world of becoming is from mechanism to spirit. Spiritual activities must manifest themselves in and through mechanical categories and conditions. We thus have the mechanical form of the spiritual manifestation and its principle of natural necessity which determines the dependence of its parts.

The first question to be settled is that of the relation of the spiritual activity to the form of necessity in which it manifests itself. Spiritual activity and freedom are identical, as we have seen, and the recognition of spiritual activity at the heart of the historic series is also the recognition of the principle of freedom at its heart. Assuming that humanity holds the principle of free activity in its bosom, the question is whether the form of necessity which mechanism imposes on its expression leaves man in possession of any actual freedom. This seems to admit of the following answer. The existence of the principle of free activity is at all events left untouched by the conditions of the problem. Man has, therefore, a principle of free activity in his nature. But the categories and laws of manifestation in this world are all mechanical, and the sphere of manifestation is dominated, therefore, by necessity. Does this effectually block freedom, or is it possible for freedom to overcome necessity?

In the chapter on Morality we have already pointed out the dualism to which this antinomy between freedom and necessity gives rise. From the moral point of view, the spiritual dialectic takes the form of a struggle of the spiritual principle to overcome mechanical necessity, and bring it into harmony with its law of freedom. This is a step toward the solution of the present difficulty. We have only to ascertain how freedom can overcome mechanism in order to make the solution complete. Now, we may concede at the outset that freedom cannot overcome mechanism by suppressing it. Such is not the mode of spiritual progress. But it may overcome by transformation. The law of the series is mechanical causation; that is, the determination of consequents through antecedent conditions. But choice, as we have seen, is self-determination, the self which determines being the empirical self. Now, if we suppose that this empirical self is the term in the series through which mechanical necessity maintains its grip on human volition, we have only to conceive that free self-activity, in the form of conscience or ideal will, is able to modify the empirical self in such a way that its determinations will gradually approximate to the requirements of the ideal law. This would mean the triumph of freedom over mechanism, not by its suppression, but by its transformation, so that while maintaining the integrity of its form, it becomes the instrument of a free spirit.

The possibility of subordinating mechanical necessity to freedom is the first and most fundamental condition of historic progress. To deny this is tantamount to denying the possibility of progress. The remaining conditions are important, but they are external. The closest of these are the biological. The spirit of man animates a corporeal organism which modifies and conditions the whole form of his existence. The biological series includes the psychological and is itself included in the cosmic. The cosmic conditions embrace man's whole physical environment external to his own organism, such as climate, soil, food, habitat.

The biologic and cosmic conditions are to be included in the plexus of mechanical forces which enter into and affect the destiny of man. The various degrees in which this influence is exerted relative to the strength of the human spirit, have doubtless much to do in determining race differences and the distinctive characteristics of different tribes or nations. Now, we may accord to these mechanical forces and agencies the full measure of influence which the most liberal construction of facts may call for, without thereby establishing any valid plea for fatalistic necessity. Fatalism rests on the presuppositions of the pure passivity of the human spirit and the absolute inflexibility of mechanical conditions. Both presuppositions are false, for, in the first place, we have seen that the very idea of spirit involves activity of the highest form. The soul of man, which is a developing spiritual activity, cannot in its nature be a mere sufferer from the mechanical forces, but must react upon them and modify them as they modify it. In the second place, mechanism is not inflexible. It is itself a modified function of a spiritual principle and is to be conceived, therefore, as holding an inner fluency within its inflexible outer form. The world-process, as we have seen, is an evolution in which an inner force passes through mechanism to higher forms of activity. The temper of mechanism is, therefore, flexible and may be moulded into a variety of shapes.

Without its presuppositions fatalism falls to the ground, and the conception of necessity that remains is one which identifies it with mechanical causation or the principle that connects phenomena with conditions out of which they arise, and thus maintains the continuity of the series. But this principle, as we have seen, only limits the freedom of spirit in this sense that it determines the form of spiritual manifestation. Mechanism and spirit are not completely antithetic terms. They rather make up a complemental dualism which expresses the potential and actual, the outer and inner of reality.

The above conception of the conditions of man's life enables us to see how the gradual evolution in and through them of a spiritual type of being is possible. If the spiritual principle in man is active it will react upon the mechanism which environs it, and if this mechanism is flexible, then it will be modified and the conditions of progress will be established. Not only so, but that very principle of continuity which enables mechanism to impose a limit upon spiritual activity is an instrument which spirit turns to its own use. For if, through it, mechanism loads its dice and predetermines results, it is always possible that the weights may be spiritual and that the outcome may be spiritual advance. The only inflexible strand in mechanical causation is that which binds every part of the series fast to the car of some antecedent. It demands that in this antecedent shall be found the determinants of what follows. But it gives no insight into the nature of these determinants. They may be mechanical agents or they may be a spiritual activity. In the psychic series the antecedent of choice is the empirical self, that is, the self with all the modifications it has inherited and acquired through its own experience. But we have seen how this empirical self is open to the constant modifying influence of an ideal spiritual force which is ever active in the human consciousness, and how, upon this activity of the ideal the possibility of an approximation of the empirical self to the ideal standard is grounded.

In the psychic series the antecedent is a fluent term and may be spiritually modified, and we have only to recognize the same essential conditions as affecting the life of humanity in order to see how the antecedent in the historic series, which is something analogous to the empirical self of the psychic series, will be always open to the modifying influence of that ideal spiritual activity which is ever energizing in the conscious experience of man. The principle of mechanical continuity may thus be made subservient to the development of spiritual freedom.

The great obstacle in the way of recognizing this

is a false idea of freedom. The only absolute freedom is that of a self-active spirit which has all the conditions of its activity within itself. That is to say, the only absolutely free being is absolute spirit. But man is not absolute spirit. He is a creature endowed with a spiritual principle, but this principle is not in a state of pure actuality, but it is rather passing perpetually from potence into actuality. This determines man as a developing being who has a history in time, and whose life is subject to mechanical conditions. The freedom of such a being cannot be absolute, but must be that which is open to a developing creature. At the centre of man's nature is a spiritual principle, which is the potency of absolute freedom. Its ideal is, therefore, absolute freedom, and this ideal is uttered in the voice of conscience. But the ideal stands as the goal of an infinite progress through mechanical conditions which modify the spiritual activity in the following manner.

Choice is self-determination, and if all the conditions of it were immanent to the self-activity that chooses, then absolute freedom would be realized. But some of the conditions of man's self-determination are external to his self-activity and enter into it, therefore, as modifying elements. Now, the empirical self that determines in choice is the self-activity thus modified. And since it is a modified self that determines, it will be a modified self that is determined. The form of absolute freedom; that is, self-determination, will be maintained in this activity, but the activity itself will be one that is modified by external and mechanical conditions. The freedom that is realized in such an activity will not be an absolute freedom, but one that is modified in various degrees by the mechanical conditions to which the spiritual activity is subject.

It is clear that the extent to which the mechanical conditions are able to modify the spiritual activity and bring it down from the plane of absolute freedom, will depend on the state of development of this spiritual activity itself, and that it will vary with this development. And here comes in the function of the ideal through which the law of perfect freedom is kept perpetually before the spirit of man, quickening it ever into higher stages of activity, and thus penetrating and modifying that mass which we call the empirical self. The presence of an ideal of freedom in the human consciousness as the goal of spiritual activity thus makes the achievement of a relative and modified freedom possible. For, while man has a spiritual principle in his nature which sets before him an ideal freedom as the law of his being, he is a developing creature and the law of his activity must be a law of becoming, that is, a law of progress. His relative freedom, the only freedom that is open to him, is achieved in an infinite and perpetual progress toward the realization of a spiritual ideal.

It is on the negative side of the problem that we hit upon the only real element of fatalism with which the destiny of man is affected. So long as we deal with positive principles and forces, we are in the sphere of progress, growth, and development. But there is a negative side to human life as well as to the world in general. We have seen in the chapter on Non-Being and Evil, that evil is a kind of eccentricity or aberration which arises out of negative grounds. These negative grounds are inevitable to creature existence and may be traced to one primal root, the absence from the creature of the principle of self-existence and its primal dependence, therefore, upon another. If we ask for the primal ground of the world we are led out of the world to its transcendent source. This negative quality of the creature constitutes its dependence, and out of its dependence springs its mutability and liability to aberration. It is true that the creative energy expresses itself in a spiritual potence in the world as the immanent principle of its development. But the immediate presupposition of this potence is the self-activity of absolute Spirit. It would otherwise be an abstraction. Now, when we represent this potentiality as gradually passing into actuality in the world-series, and as finally becoming the norm of conscious spiritual life in the soul of man, we do not in reality bring in a mediatory principle between the Creator and the world, but we rather indicate the mode in which absolute self-activity can be conceived as becoming the creative energy of an imperfect and dependent world. The world could not be the immediate phenomenon of the Absolute without being absolute itself. But as the gradual product of absolute energy conceived as going out into the negative sphere in the form of spiritual potence, the rise of a real world which is yet absolutely dependent on a transcendent ground becomes intelligible.

If now we suppose the world-series to become self-conscious at any point, as it does in the soul of man, we can well understand that its consciousness will not be that of the Absolute, but rather a creature consciousness which, through the same process by which it becomes conscious of itself, will also arrive at the consciousness of the absolute ground on which it depends. Some such reflection as this must have been in the mind of Descartes when he affirmed a necessary connection between man's idea of himself and his idea of God, and further conceived the idea of God to be the presupposition of man's self-consciousness. Descartes must have felt dimly what may be apprehended more clearly; namely, that what we have called the ideal self in man or the psychic logos, is the immediate organ of man's intuition or intimation of the Absolute whom his spirit calls Father. And since this ideal self contains the norms of our conceptions of absolute goodness, beauty, and truth, the spontaneous synthesis in which our consciousness binds these with the idea of God and represents God as the ideal good of man, is the true voice of a profound reason.

To return now from a seeming digression: We have said that it is on the negative side of the problem that we hit upon the only element of fatalism with which the destiny of man is affected. This can now be verified. If fatalism enters our world at all, it comes in through the door of evil. We have seen that evil is aberration, or departure of any creature from its normal orbit which represents its good. It is only when the creature is in its normal position, fulfilling the true law of its being, that the world is friendly to it and presents itself as a sphere of order, law, and development. If it wanders from its true path, the forces which before were propitious become hostile and do it harm. What was before a sphere of order becomes one of cross purposes and caprice. To the wandering planet the world is out of joint and cosmos has been turned into chaos. Evil enters as an active force into the destiny of man through the will. The normal choice of the human will is the ideal good, and the normal pathway of its orbit is toward its realization. This is true however we may conceive the ideal good, whether as an ideal spiritual self or as God. Evil enters into the life of such a being when it departs from its true orbit and chooses some other guide than the law of conscience which is the law of the ideal, or when, in the extreme case, it says to evil "be thou my good." The soul that thus chooses has wrenched itself from its true orbit and become a wanderer in the moral universe. The forces which made for good when it was in its true plane, now make for evil. The vision of the soul becomes distorted and it can no longer see truth or beauty. Its will having lost its ideal guide, yields itself to passion and caprice. The stars seem to fight against it, and it gradually sinks into the pit of darkness and "primal eldest chaos."

If we generalize this representation we will reach the idea of evil as a negative factor in human progress. The ills of humanity do not all spring from normal causes. The worst of them are the fruits of an abnormal force. Evil enters the human series as a depravity of will, it leads to a degradation of character and type. It acts as a disturbing factor, creating disorder, strife, warfare and devastation. It is the principle of hate instead of love, of chaos instead of cosmos, of stagnation instead of healthful activity, of dissolution instead of development, of death instead of life.

We have now reached a point from which it is possible to obtain a general conception of the conditions of historic progress. There are two main factors in the historic stream, one positive, the other negative. The positive factor includes all the positive forces, spiritual and mechanical. The negative is the force of evil. The positive forces are conditions of development and determine the onward movements of the race. Central among these, functions the activity of the human spirit. But this spiritual activity, as we saw, is conditioned and modified in various modes and degrees by the mechanical forces which surround and affect it. These forces themselves are not, however, inflexible and fatalistic in their nature and tendency, but are fluent and flexible, and while determining the empirical form of the spiritual life of humanity, are open to the modifying and moulding influences of spiritual laws. The result of the synthesis of the spiritual and mechanical forces is the possibility of a movement of spiritual evolution toward an ideal which may be characterized as the gradual realization of human freedom.

The great foe to this movement of spiritual evolution, as we have seen, is evil, which having its negative grounds in non-being, is ever tending toward non-being. Evil enters the humanistic stream through the inlet of will. It is a capricious, fatalistic force, opposing and destroying the work of the positive principles, and acting ever as a disintegrative, dissolutive agent. The principle of evil is the motive force of disturbance, disorder, anarchy and chaos. It is the one irreconcilable foe of freedom, the one baleful, demoniac spirit which ever dogs the footsteps of life with the shadow of death.

The laws of historic progress are to be determined in view of the nature and conditions of the historic series. We do not mean by laws, in this connection, the particular forces which enter into the historic movement. These are all included in the conditions of the movement. By law is here meant mode or method, and when we seek the laws of the historic movement we are looking for the categories that will adequately represent it as a whole.

Now, it is possible to advance two radically different theories in explanation of the same fact. The historic series may be subsumed under either the category of mechanical causation or that of self-determining will. The first alternative will give rise to the necessarian, and in some cases fatalistic, theories in which all things are conceived to be strictly predetermined by mechanical conditions, and no place is left for freedom. The second alternative leads to the denial of necessity and the ascription of everything to a self-determining agent. Freedom, therefore, reigns supreme and the tendency is to ignore the claims of mechanism.

But we have seen in the preceding analysis that no such short and easy methods are possible. The fact we have to deal with is two-sided, and its explanation is one which must in some way effect a synthesis of mechanism and freedom. How this is to be done may be suggested by the insight we have already obtained into the nature and conditions of the historic series. In the light of all the elements that enter into it, the whole significance of the historic movement is expressed in the idea of a progressive struggle of the human spirit toward the realization of ideal freedom. In the progress itself consists the actual freedom that is open to a developing creature.

Now, if we confine our attention to the positive factors, the fact that presents itself is a dialectic interaction between spiritual and mechanical forces, in which progress is made when the spiritual forces are able to dominate and modify the mechanical. If we suppose this to be uniformly the case and also assume the constancy of the forces, the result will be a straight-forward and gradual process of spiritual evolution. But nowhere does such a movement appear, and this because neither of our suppositions is strictly true. In the history of the race it is not true that the spiritual forces have uniformly dominated, or that the interacting forces have remained constant. Given a particular combination of mechanical forces, as for example the environment of a particular nation or race, and it may be assumed that the operation of these will be fairly uniform. But the spiritual forces show a disposition to ebb and flow. The human spirit is mysteriously seized by some inspiration and the force of its energy sweeps everything before it. Again, some paralysis seems to fall on the spirit of a people, and there follow an atrophy of spiritual activities and a lapse to a lower stratum of development.

So our expectation of even-paced progress is disappointed, and instead we find a dual movement in which the fruits of development seem to be ever falling into the jaws of dissolution. The truth is, the positive forces never act alone, but the whole drama has its negative side. There is in the world a tendency to non-being which makes it necessary for the evolution philosopher to couple with his category of development that of dissolution. Progress is made through the triumph of integrative over disintegrative forces. But at length equilibrium is reached, a period of stagnation ensues, and then the destructive forces take the lead in the race and the whole labor of the builders is gradually undone. This is the picture in the sphere of mechanical forces.

Where the spiritual forces enter the fact is not altered, but it requires different interpretation. Upon the mechanical dialectic which still goes on is superimposed a dialectic of spirit. Mechanism affects spirit not externally but through spirit itself. All the conditions, positive and negative, are translated into spiritual effect and become immanent in the spiritual struggle.

Thus arises a law of duality which brings the whole movement under the categories of development and dissolution. The forces of growth and organization prevail for a time and we have the phenomena of human progress, of nations developing in power and civilization, of races moving on to a splendid destiny. But a time comes when the forces of negation which have been held in solution assert themselves, paralysis of energy ensues and then the sinews of the people's strength begin to rot under the corroding influence of vice, their faith bows to scepticism, the rich fabrics which they have built with the travail of their spirit dissolve and, amid the ruins of the once fair tenement of their spirit, courage fails and hope sinks into the night of despair.

The world thus seems to be a monster that swallows up all its own children. The baleful spell of evil and negation seems to have destroyed our fair vision of a humanity rising gradually into the light of freedom and thrown the shadow of fatalism over the whole scene. This would be the logical conclusion were not a higher interpretation of the human story possible, which enables us to see light through the darkness and to bind again the broken threads of continuity.

The true method of history can be best apprehended, we think, by conceiving the origin in individual form, of reservoirs of stored-up spiritual energy which stand at the beginning of each new epoch. We may represent a new increment of conscious spiritual force as being generated in these reservoirs and as supplying the living inspiration of a new culture. The new movement may be local, national, or racial; its history will be that of the struggle of a new ideal, partial as it ordinarily is, to transform the empirical conditions in which it energizes, into new and higher forms. The struggle will under normal conditions be successful until the potential of the primal inspiration has been exhausted. Then the forces of the negative will begin to dominate and a movement will set in toward dissolution and death.

Now, there is no natural reason why the movement of decay should not end in dissolution and bring historic evolution to a close. And this would inevitably happen, we think, did not the historic individual or group, in which the new order is initiated, bear a peculiar relation to the old. The rise of prophets of new dispensations is coincident with the deep decline of the old. When the destructive forces are most rampant and the spiritual world in which man has lived crumbles about his ears, hope is crushed and the spiritual consciousness is thrown back violently upon itself. It is this violent backflow of spiritual reaction that precedes new incarnations of organizing force and the incoming of a new and higher ideal in the consciousness of some historic individual. There appears on earth then a new hero, perhaps a new martyr, the founder of a new movement, or a spiritual regenerator of the order that is dying out.

This back-flow of the spiritual consciousness upon itself, caused by a deep sense of the prevalence of death and dissolution, is a necessary condition of the birth of new spiritual forces and ideals. But it alone will not explain the result. The reactionary wave is one of despair and in itself will produce only the skeptical pessimist who gives up the struggle and escapes the anguish of it by a plunge into non-being, or the stoic who stubbornly resists in the inner citadel of his personality, the onset of despair and when his dearest hopes are dead " orders his stout heart to bear it." But it is only when the back-flow is met and overcome by some Divine inflow of new spiritual energy, that the historic individual is born and the stoic is transformed into the hero-martyr of a new dispensation.

In order, then, to conceive the true fortunes of the struggle for spiritual freedom in human history, we must modify our concept of fatalistic evolution and decay by this idea of an epochal inflow of spiritual force which embodies itself in the consciousness of some historic individual or group, in whom it becomes the living energy of new ideals of life and culture, and in whom also it stands related to the dissolutive stages of the old order, checking its reaction of spiritual despair by that inflowing wave of new Divine force which brings to light new spheres of ideal spiritual life.

This intuition enables us to restore the broken threads of continuity and to see how the pathway of humanity may through all its vicissitudes be upward toward the light. But it contains a presupposition; namely, the inability of the race to conserve its own development and its dependence on some power that transcends it for the renovation of its springs of spiritual energy. For, just as we discovered in the sphere of the individual life, the necessary function of a psychic logos which at the same time supplies an ideal spiritual force to its development and binds it in a living bond to the being that transcends it; so here, in the broader sphere of the universal life of humanity, we come upon the necessity for a historic logos which shall at the same time supply the race with its advancing spiritual ideals and bind it with an indefectible bond to that absolute fountain of spiritual energy to which it owes the continuity of its life.

XIII

RELIGION

Religion is the highest spiritual outcome of the common life of humanity. Its spring is that historic logos in which there is a functional union of man's spiritual nature with the absolute Spirit which is its presupposition. It is in this synthetic spring that religion has its primal source. An intuition of this fact enables us to understand, as we could not otherwise do, the religious phenomena of the race. Man's religious consciousness, even in its lowest forms and whatever be the circumstances and conditions of its rise, holds in it a sense, however vague, of some power that transcends it, upon which it depends, and with which it needs to be at peace. The conscience of man, instinctively at first and reflectively afterward, identifies this power with the source of its own ideal life, and thus the object of the religious consciousness becomes also the ideal of supreme good.

Religion thus includes the ethic springs in which, as we have seen, are contained the norms of the social and civic life of man. And this explains, we think, the universal fact that all social and civic life and organization are historically grounded in religious soil. For religion is the faith by which the spirit of man maintains its vital connection with the transcendent ground of its existence and activity, and this faith, however rudimental it may be, constitutes the medium in which man's whole life is unified and developed.

But we are specially interested at this point, not so much in the historic aspect of religion as in its nature and the grounds on which it rests. The idea of religion presupposes certain structural conceptions treated of in former chapters; namely, the ideas of absolute being, the world-process as related to its absolute ground, and the human soul. Without some rational notions of these it will be impossible to conceive either the grounds out of which the religious consciousness arises or the fundamental problems it has to solve.

Religion rests on a dual relation of distinction and synthesis between the human soul and its absolute ground. This connection can be rendered intelligible only when we conceive the Absolute as spirit, that is, as self-conscious personal being. This absolute Spirit, energizing in the outer negative sphere, generates the world which is to be conceived as the product of a transcendent spiritual cause and as containing the potence of spiritual development in it as the immanent principle of its activity. This potence, which is nothing independent of the Absolute, represents the mode in which the creative force generates a developing and dependent sphere of reality. It actualizes itself in the world-process, passing up from mechanism to spiritual actuality, which it first achieves in the soul of man.

The human soul is thus the highest actualization of the spiritual potence that is immanent in the world. But the human soul is not complete actuality. In it the unfolding world-energy has become conscious, and it is, therefore, a being that is ever passing out of potence into actuality. This constitutes its activity a ceaseless evolution, the infinite good of which is completely actualized spirit.

Upon this basis, as we have seen, rises the soul's dual consciousness and life. Its activity is a dualistic dialectic, a passage from mechanism to spirit and in its consciousness experience is a species of dialectic between an empirically limited and modified self and an ideal self which we have called the psychic logos. This logos functions as a spiritual ideal which contains the norms of perfection and imposes its ethical law upon the soul as its unconditional standard of duty. We have seen, also, how this psychic logos spheres out into the historic logos in the universal life of humanity, and how this historic logos becomes the special organ of religion.

In order, however, to determine truly the nature and grounds of religion, there is a special factor which must be taken into account, and that is the existence of evil. We have in another place endeavored to theorize evil as a factor of reality. Here the point of interest is its bearing on the conditions with which religion has to deal. This, however, is a difficult problem whose solution involves a rational insight into the nature of the relation that subsists between the soul of man and the Absolute, since on our conception of this relation hangs our whole theory of the nature of evil. Now, in the light of conceptions already achieved we are led to view the relation as being necessarily one of consciously distinct individualities. The Absolute can be conceived only as *purus actus* or completely actualized spirit, and its consciousness will consequently be that of complete and self-realized individuality, while the human soul is ever passing from potence to actuality in the stages of an evolution, and its consciousness is that of an imperfect, developing creature. The synthesis is the function of the logos. This is one of the hardest points in religious philosophy; namely, to realize how the ideal which imposes its law upon the soul, functions also as the organ of religion. It is necessary, however, to master it in order to become competent to deal with the most vital issues of religious theory. When we posit a synthesis between the human soul and the Absolute in the logos, we do not assert the ultimate identity of the two. There is an identity of essence, since both are spiritual activities. But there is not identity of individuality, of consciousness, or of personality. The individualities are distinct in that, while both are unitary, the Absolute is self-comprehended in an eternal circle, while the human ego is related to an empirical stream which it is ever gathering up into knots, but never completely comprehending. The consciousnesses and personalities are distinct for analogous reasons, because in man they are functions of imperfect, developing activities which determine their distinctive characteristics, while the consciousness and personality of the Absolute are absolute and, therefore, incapable of development.

The synthesis involved must then mean something other than identity. It is a common experience in imparting instruction, that the thoughts which are perfectly comprehended in the mind of the master are able to penetrate the consciousness of the pupil, even when they are very imperfectly understood. In such case they are only seeds planted, which must spring up and ripen before they are capable of becoming in the mind of the pupil what they are in that of the master. Now, we may find in this experience of the interaction of minds a key to the connection between the Absolute and the human soul, in the logos. It is possible that the contents of the absolute consciousness may enter the human consciousness as norms of a perfection which it only dimly comprehends, and the reasonableness of this supposition is borne out by the fact that man has in conscience such anticipations of a perfection that he does not understand, but which at the same time presses on him as the ideal law of his nature.

We conceive, then, that in the consciousness of the ideal self or psychic logos, there is such a synthesis of the Absolute and the soul of man as enables the

Absolute to communicate its own thought to the human consciousness as the norm of ideal truth, and its own will or volition as the norm or law of an ideal good. We conceive, in short, the existence of such a synthesis as makes the inflow of the Absolute's thought and energy into the channels of human spiritual activity not only possible but rational and probable.

The result we obtain from this, perhaps oversubtle, disquisition, is the concept of the human soul as a being distinct in its conscious individuality and in the type of its activity, from the absolute Spirit, while it is yet, through its logos-consciousness, in close and effective connection with it. And this brings us to the point where the bearing of evil on the religious problem can be most clearly seen. If the individuality of the soul is distinct from that of the Absolute, then the will of the soul is also distinct and it has the power of individual choice. But we have seen that the ideal perfection of the soul consists in thinking what the Absolute thinks and willing what the Absolute wills. The soul has a distinct will, however, and may use it to dethrone the Absolute from the place of the ideal and to put some inferior and creature good in its place. Thus evil will originate in the soul and aberration or departure from its normal orbit will follow, with all the consequences which have been detailed in the preceding chapter.

The effect of this fall into evil, in the religious sphere, will be twofold. In the first place, it will produce within the soul a depravation of will and a consequent corruption of the whole nature. In the dualistic struggle between the positive and negative forces of good and evil, the negative will gain the ascendancy and the soul will set out on a downward road. In the second place, it will produce what we may call a *typal* defection, namely, a fall from God. The distinction between the soul and its absolute ground will widen into a breach and the difference of will and consciousness will become a gulf and the soul will become possessed with a painful sense of its distance and alienation from God. Accompanying this sense of alienation will be a deepening experience of the disturbance of the normal emotional relation of the soul to God. The sense of harmony and of the Divine favor will be exchanged for a growing feeling of discordance and a deepening sense of the Divine wrath, and under the weight of the sense of its own fall from the path of the ideal and its own consequent demerit, a load of conscious guilt will begin to weigh it down, until instead of a joyful bathing of the soul in the light of God's countenance, there will be a fearful looking for of Divine judgment.

The primal sense of religious need is founded in the nature of man as an imperfect creature whose progressive life must consist in a development of his spiritual potencies into actuality. We have seen in the last chapter that humanity has not the power in itself to conserve its own development, but that the springs of its strength are in the Absolute. Man is, therefore, both a growing and a dependent creature, and out of this springs his sense and his need of religion. The primal function of religion, therefore, is to subserve the spiritual evolution of man by binding his soul fast to the absolute source of its strength, and by opening it to the inflow of the Divine grace through the channel of unifying love. But this *religious need is intensified and made more urgent by evil.* The moral degradation of the soul under the sense of its fall becomes a conviction of sin, and the feeling of guilt and the consequent anticipation of the Divine wrath are all experiences arising from the soul's aberration from the normal of its true orbit. In view of them the religious need becomes not simply spiritual development and communion with God but redemption, regeneration, restoration from a fall, atonement and pardon.

Conceiving the need of religion as thus intensified by the existence of evil and its effects in the spiritual world, we see that the problem of religion is profounder than that of simple morality. It is true that religion must conserve morality, but this arises not from the identity of religion with morality, but from the fact that religion includes morality. The moral intuition conceives spiritual renovation and the evolution of man from the inner standpoint of conscience. In conscience the ideal law of the soul's higher self is revealed and moral progress consists in the gradual approximation of the empirical self to the standard of the ideal. The moral drama is, therefore, the inner drama of conscience as an autonomous force. The religious intuition goes deeper. It sees that conscience can be autonomous only so far as the Absolute functions in it and causes it to think the divine thoughts and utter in its legislation the divine will. Only thus, by becoming the voice of God, does conscience become the organ of an ideal law and, therefore, autonomous. Religion recognizes the fact that conscience may become perverted by turning away from the primal source of its inspiration and becoming either self-willed and trusting to its own inner light, or placing some inferior and creature good upon the throne of the ideal. Religion says, therefore, that the primal need of all, which underlies the moral, and the satisfaction of which is the precondition of moral good, is the soul's recognition of its dependence on God and its need of a life in union with his.

Man is an individual with a conscience and a moral ideal to realize. He is also a type of being standing in relation to the absolute ground of his existence and toward which the normal law of his being tends in an upward spiritual progress. He has, therefore, a typal destiny before him, the achievement of unity with the divine life. In view of the issues evil has created in the experience of our race, both the moral and typal problems have become more grave and more urgent. The synthesis of religion must include both. It must conserve moral renovation and development; it must also conserve the typal need by leading man back to God and keeping ever alive in him the consciousness of his divine relationship.

The conclusions we come to here enable us to interpret another element which stands central in religious experience and connects it with the profoundest law of historic progress. It has already appeared that humanity is not able to conserve its own spiritual evolution, but must seek the springs of its power in the Absolute. From this point of view the energy of the Absolute must be conveyed into the channels of human activity, and hence arises the necessity for mediation. Historic progress in general, as we saw, is mediated by the appearance of historic characters and groups, through whom the spiritual supply is introduced from the Absolute into the human sphere. These historic individuals or groups thus serve as reservoirs of a stored-up spiritual energy which gradually permeates the mass of humanity and constitutes the inspiration of a new national development, or it may be, a new chapter in civilization. This law of mediation finds its most important and momentous application in the sphere of religion. The profoundest root of religion is, as we have seen, the synthesis of the human consciousness with the Divine in the historic logos, and out of this root springs also the deepest issue of religion; namely, the typal union of the soul with God as the primal condition of all spiritual and moral good.

Since, then, religion is concerned with the springs and roots of all spiritual life and development, it is to be expected that this spiritual law of mediation will have its most momentous application in the religious sphere. Every historic personage through whom a real advance is made in human progress is a mediator, and every group or nation which adds a chapter to the spiritual evolution of humanity is the bearer of an inspiration which it has received from a higher source. But the mediator may not be conscious of his mission. The historic logos may use the individual or the nation for the accomplishment of a purpose which the agent does not realize. This has been finely portrayed by Shakespeare in the historical plays. Julius Cæsar, as the incarnation of the imperial spirit, rides triumphantly into power over the ruins of the Republic, although his own reflection shows little other motive than personal ambition. Again, in the English series, Bolingbroke is able to destroy the old monarchy and introduce a new chapter in English history, because he is the bearer of the new national spirit, although he shows little consciousness of the mission he is realizing and is dominated, in the main, by somewhat paltry personal aims. The historic logos employs unconscious and, it may be, hostile instruments to accomplish its purposes, and history will be studied without discernment if the wide and important scope of this unwitting mediational function be not recognized. For there is a true sense in which the logos overrules all things, and even the wrath of wicked men is made to subserve the ends of good.

But the religious mediator is one who is conscious of his spiritual mission. Whether he be the founder of a new dispensation or a prophet and reformer of an old one, he must feel himself to be the mouthpiece and organ of the Supreme Power. He must be God's man, and speak and act as he is moved by the Holy Ghost. He may be mistaken and the light that is in him may be mingled with darkness, but he must always be the conscious organ of a spiritual power that is higher than himself. Every new religion and every great reform, or revival of an old religion, is mediated by such a historic individual or group, and the new spiritual impulse that is thus communicated to the race will have a power to mould and elevate humanity that is proportioned to the spiritual purity and elevation of its organ.

The mediation effected may, however, be only relative and incomplete. The historic individual may found a new dispensation, as Mohammed did, without himself claiming divine honors or becoming an object of religious worship. The historic mediator may simply regard himself as God's prophet. He may be conscious simply of speaking as he is moved by the Holy Ghost, and although in performing this function he may found a new religion or introduce a new spiritual content into one that already exists, his function will be different from that of a mediator who is also the Christ. This will appear if we determine what the Christ-function is and what it implies. The historic logos is the medium through which all spiritual truth comes to man. Now, the primal ground of spiritual communication in this medium is a synthesis of the divine and the human, in which the divine spirit informs the human spirit with energies that inspire it, but which the human spirit only partly apprehends. The prophet is the man who realizes this mode of divine communication in his consciousness, and is inspired by it to the utterance of new truth.

There is conceivable, however, a higher consciousness than this; namely, the *consciousness of the synthesis itself*. The logos, as we have seen, is that organ in which the norms of perfection are revealed, conscience giving the revelation on the ethical side. These norms imperfectly apprehended by the human spirit, are recognized as lineaments of an absolute consciousness in which they are completely realized. Could the logos now completely realize its content, there would appear a soul in which the consciousness of the synthesis would arise and it would feel itself to be both human and divine. There is no contradiction involved in the conception of such a nature. It is in fact the logical outcome of the idea of creation developed in the chapters on Being and Non-Being and Becoming. We there reached the conception of the world as the product of the logos-energy of the Absolute. But the world rises to spiritual consciousness in the human soul and this soul has immanent in it the consciousness of an ideal which it cannot fully realize and this ideal, conceived as completely actualized, is also its idea of absolute spirit. The ideal thus mediates between the soul and the Absolute, entering on the one side into the developing series of the temporal life and on the other side resting in the eternal blessedness of the Absolute. In it the teleological idea of the creation is therefore realized.

The synthetic consciousness which thus arises is that of the Christ as distinguished from the religious prophet. It is a consciousness in which an ideal harmony or atonement is established between the divine and the human. It is a consciousness in which the typal gulf is perpetually closed and unity is restored by the entering of the soul into the sonship of God and the reciprocal passage of the divine Father spirit into the soul as God in the Christ, reconciling the world to himself.

The Christ, then, is the ideal mediator between God and the human spirit. There may be prophets without number, who embody the divine inspiration, and founders of new dispensations which mark decided spiritual advances of the race. But as there is only one God and one perfect ideal for humanity, it is not conceivable that there should be more than one perfect type of mediation. The historic individual in whom this perfect type is embodied, will stand, therefore, as the Christ of the race. He will be the founder of the perfect universal religion of the spirit, which will ideally meet every need and become the great spiritual fountain-light for all humanity.

The above analysis supplies criteria by which various religious conceptions may be judged. Of these conceptions the leading at the present day are mysticism, agnosticism, positivism, the moralistic theory of Kant, and the absolutism of the school of Hegel. Mysticism is an element in true as well as false religion. Its truth consists in the fact that the soul, through the organ of the logos, becomes inspired with truth which it can only imperfectly understand. It is compelled, therefore, to resort to symbols and imagery which present in concrete vision what the reason is able only partially to translate. Mysticism becomes false when it attempts to substitute its symbols for completely rationalized conceptions. The two historic embodiments of this misuse of mysticism are Hindu pantheism and the Theosophy of Jacob Böhme. Hindu pantheism starts with the conception of the nothingness of the relative or phenomenal world and reaches with a bound the idea of the Absolute as the unitary negation of this nothingness, an unthinkable Nirvana into which everything falls and is lost. Jacob Böhme starts with the conception of absolute being as a chaos of struggling and heterogeneous elements, light and darkness, life and death, good and evil, out of which a dualistic world gradually emerges.

Neither of these forms of mysticism are able, however, to arrive consistently at true religious conceptions. Hindu pantheism, through its negative idea of the Absolute, can achieve nothing but an ideal which swallows up the human spirit, and it can found no religious discipline, therefore, except a prescription for self-annihilation. The Böhmistic scheme fails also, but in a somewhat different way.

Through its confusion of being and non-being in one conception, it is unable to achieve any rational or coherent ideas of the world. The result is a species of intellectual chaos out of which the profoundly religious feeling of Böhme is able to elicit only the semblance of order.

Agnosticism is the theory that postulates the existence of an unintelligible absolute as the ground of the world. It clings to the transcendent idea of religion, but because the absolute nature is inconceivable it finds itself unable to realize any *nexus* between the Absolute and the relative. This deprives it of any intelligible basis for religion and it is compelled to fall back on the sense of mystery as the sole content of the religious consciousness. This is tantamount to defecating the religious idea of both its moral and typal significance. The agnostic may then speak of reverence and worship, but these sentiments can only be called forth by moral and spiritual attributes. The logic of agnosticism in the end reduces the whole religious problem to an enigma which it is compelled to give up.

Positivism eliminates the Absolute from its religious conceptions altogether and seeks to find in humanity a satisfying object for the religious consciousness. Its idea of man is also a purely naturalistic one, from which all spiritual elements are eliminated. There is, thus, no spiritual foundation left to build on and what it proposes is not religion, but a substitute that fails to satisfy most of the profounder demands of the religious consciousness.

Of the moralistic theory of religion Kant is the ablest exponent. "Religion Within the Limits of Pure Reason" is almost the greatest modern philosophical treatise on religion. It is founded on a fine intuition of the dualistic nature of man's moral consciousness. The indwelling in man of opposing principles of good and evil is posited as the ground of an everlasting moral struggle. And this struggle supplies the basis, on the humanistic side, for a doctrine of the atonement made by Jesus Christ, through which is secured the victory of the good over the evil and the establishment of a kingdom of God on earth. Here is a moral conception which leads us to expect much when the philosopher takes up the consideration of the transcendent aspect of his problem. But here Kant strikes the limits of his philosophy. The root of the difficulty is his failure, in dealing with the metaphysical side of the problem of knowledge, to reach any adequate notion of the nature of God or any solid assurance of his existence. His failure here cuts him off from any rational doctrine of transcendence, a failure which is not retrieved in his moral postulates. For these simply assert as moral necessities, but without any additional speculative insight, the fundamental data of religion; namely, the existence of God as a transcendent being and the freedom and immortality of the soul. And depending absolutely on moral grounds for their validity, the data of religion must be subordinated to the data of morality. The result of this failure to assert any real transcendence is that religion is virtually reduced to a humanistic basis. Kant's theory of religion is fine on its ethical side, but its speculative blindness causes it to miss or adumbrate many of the basal ideas and distinctions on which an adequate philosophy of religion must be grounded.

Absolutism in religion is represented by the Hegelian school. Hegel's intuition strikes deeper than Kant's, and obtains a fuller and firmer grasp of spiritual reality. For a conception of the internal movement of spiritual activity and of the living process of absolute spirit, Hegelism alone, of modern systems, supplies an effective clue. But Hegel fails in one cardinal point of religious theory. He is never able to differentiate absolute spirit from the spirit of man. This weakness arises, as we have seen in an earlier chapter, from his failure to achieve a true doctrine of the negative. This alone enables us to conceive the modification that constitutes the differentia of relativity and consequently the differentia of the human soul. Not being able to differentiate the Absolute from the conscious activity in man, Hegel sees no other way of defining religion than as the consciousness which the Absolute has of itself. This is virtually to annul the human spirit as a distinct individuality, and, as we have seen, this would suppress the basal relation out of which the religious consciousness arises.

This difficulty appears very clearly, in a somewhat different form, in a recent work by a distinguished member of the school.[1] The primal distinction in

[1] Evolution of Religion—Edward Caird.

consciousness, this author reasons, is that between subject and object. But this dualism is reduced to unity by a higher bond. This bond which unifies subject and object is God, and the unitary consciousness is what Hegel would call the Absolute's consciousness of himself. This doctrine has far-reaching consequences in the work alluded to, for it virtually assumes that God and the principle of unity are one and the same. The author so understands it, and when the question of God's relation to the world-process arises he flatly denies all transcendence and identifies God completely with the immanent principle of the world's evolution.

The truth is, we find a common microbe at work here and in old Hegelism. For the unitary bond which is here identified with the Absolute is the common possession of all self-conscious spiritual beings. That fact, however, is consistent with the existence of distinct consciousnesses, individualities, and wills, and these constitute the real distinctions in the spiritual world. What this author calls God is an abstraction, for it is what is left of spirit when all distinctive characteristics have been abstracted from. The idea of the unitary bond is the bare idea of spiritual substance. And it is clear that when this abstract notion of spiritual substance is mistaken for the idea of God, the thinker who commits the mistake will be in a dilemma similar to that of Spinoza, and there will be no escape from a species of naturalistic pantheism.

An adequate conception of the historic evolution

of religion is possible only in view of the true data of religion. These, as we have seen, are (1) a transcendent Absolute whose energy functions creatively in the world as an immanent spiritual principle or potency; (2) the human soul a spiritual principle passing perpetually from potence to actuality and thus epitomizing the world-progress from mechanism up to actualized spirit; (3) the logos which functions immanently as man's ideal law-giver and transcendently as the organ of divine communication to the human soul. It thus becomes the organ of the religious consciousness. Out of these conditions the evolution of religion arises. No evolution is conceivable on a purely naturalistic basis; much less an evolution of religion, for, as we have seen, all world-progress is the function of a spiritual potence and the immediate presupposition of this potence is a transcendent actuality. Now, the religious consciousness involves this presupposition raised to its highest power, since it is the organ of man's highest, that is, his ideal spirituality, and springs out of the function of the logos, which is the point of immediate spiritual communion between the human and the divine. The very existence of this communion involves the idea of an absolute spiritual energy transcending in its conscious individuality and will the human spirit with which it communicates. And the evolution of religion is the direct function of this inter-communion which is the spring of a developing spirituality and of an evolving religious consciousness.

The law of religious evolution is also that law of general spiritual progress which we have developed in the preceding chapter, raised to its highest power. That law is founded on the presupposition of an inter-communion between the human spirit and its transcendent ground. Its operation is conditioned, as we have seen, by two circumstances of profound import. One is the inter-dependence of the transcendent and immanent agencies in determining the stages of the evolution. It has been pointed out how the appearance of the prophet or founder of a new dispensation is conditioned on the one hand by a back-flowing wave of spiritual despair and on the other, by an inflow of new spiritual energy from the absolute spring. The juncture and inter-action of the immanent and transcendent forces, thus produces the spiritual embodiment of a new advance in the religious progress of humanity. The other circumstance is the inter-play of evil with the forces of good. Evil is an omnipresent fact and contingency in the world and it functions as an adversary, as a principle of degeneration, rotting spiritual fibre and producing an ever-active tendency to dissolution and death. We have seen how active moral evil arises as an effect of the human will wresting itself from the divine and embarking on its own resources. It thus attempts to ignore or cancel one of the profoundest negative laws of human experience; namely, man's inability, either as an individual or as a race, to conserve his own spiritual evolution. The option of the evil will cuts the divine branch on which humanity rests and the inevitable tendency is a gravitation downward toward spiritual death. The operation of evil thus complicates and intensifies the situation and gives to the whole spiritual history of humanity the appearance of an evolution which is constantly being swallowed up in dissolution.

It is only in the light of the true law of spiritual progress that the outlook becomes more hopeful. The spiritual ocean may on its surface seem a stagnant pool covered with the débris of dead and decaying religions and civilizations. But beneath are the currents that conserve its life and enable it to throw off the miasma of death. These embody themselves in new spiritual reservoirs which supply the energy of a new national development or civilization. And since experience teaches us that the absolute springs require many human vessels and that it is not given to the same nature or line of historic individuals to be the bearers of the highest inspirations in art, literature, philosophy or civil government, so we must bear the same lesson in mind in our search for the true steps of religious evolution. We must look for the nations and lines of prophets which are the bearers of the highest religious inspiration and which embody, therefore, the gulf-stream of spiritual history. The fortunes of the movement which embodies the highest religious experience of the race, will not include the whole record of religious evolution, nor will it enable us to ignore the inferior lights of other movements in spiritual history, but it will mark the line of greatest intensity, the points where the religious forces converge, and where the highest issues of the spiritual drama of the race are decided.

We may expect also that the race mediator and the race religion, if they are to be born into the world, will appear in connection with this supreme movement. For if spirit finds it necessary to concentrate its energies into special lines in order to produce the master-results in other spheres of race-progress, much more shall we expect that in this highest sphere of its energizing the same law will apply and that the embodiment of the supreme ideal of the religious consciousness of the race will emerge in historic form at the flood-tide of the gulf-stream of spiritual experience. That the spirit of man requires but one ideal mediator is clear. That the embodiment of such a mediator must be the supreme effort of spiritual evolution seems no less clear. And from this it seems to follow with convincing force that but one such embodiment is possible to a race, and that in this it achieves the ideal basis of its universal religion.

The religious theory of evolution posits as its primal ground a transcendent and absolute spirit whose creative energy is the presupposition of the spiritual potence of the world. It posits a world-process which passes from mechanism to spirit, and which has for its immanent ground a spiritual potence that contains the forms of relative being. It posits a human soul which is a spiritual potence passing into actuality, and which in its experience epitomizes the world-process through which its self-conscious individuality has been achieved. It posits in this soul an immanent ideal which energizes as the main-spring of its moral and spiritual activity and as the logos in which it is individually and historically united to its transcendent spiritual ground and which functions, therefore, as the spring of its religious consciousness and life. It posits on this basis a religious evolution in which, through the divine agency and assistance manifesting itself through the law of spiritual mediation, the race presses upward toward God its Father. And it posits as the supreme point of this movement, as appearing at a supreme crisis in spiritual history, the ideal mediator and the founder of the universal religion of humanity. This ideal mediator is the incarnation of the consciousness of the logos in which God is manifest, reconciling the world to himself. This is the highest, the ideal outcome of the world's spiritual history. The religious theory of evolution thus posits a divine process which, as begun, continued and ended rests upon God, but a process which cannot be pantheistically conceived, since in its inception, in every step of its progress, and in its ideal culmination in the logos, a real distinction is grounded and maintained between the creation and the absolute spirit to whose energy it owes its being.

XIV

ART

A true Metaphysic of Art can be achieved only in the light of the categories of being, non-being, and becoming. We have already seen how these ideas supply a basis for a structural ontology of theoretic and practical philosophy. They will be found equally effective in helping us to arrive at a rational theory of art.

There are three categories in the philosophy of art which must be kept distinct; namely, Art Creation, Art Representation, and Art Appreciation. The highest category is that of art creation. In dealing with it, it will be necessary, as in the treatment of morality and theoretic science, to distinguish between absolute and relative and to seek the first norms of art in the bosom of absolute being.

In the chapter on Morality, we followed the dialectic of the absolute spirit through stages of intellection and volition to that of love, which includes both and proceeds under the category of unity to realize wholeness or completeness of being. And we saw how out of this unifying impulse of the Absolute spring the norms both of the moral idea of holiness and the æsthetic idea of beauty. Now, back of this impulse lies the concrete spiritual activity itself, which in this relation we may call the artistic intelligence, which is to be conceived on one side as a sense for unity and on the other, in Mathew Arnold's phrase, as a sense for beauty. We will have, in short, the idea of an intelligence that apprehends and grasps all parts and details mediately through the idea of the whole from the contemplation of which it also derives an æsthetic satisfaction.

If we apprehend rightly the nature of art-intelligence we have a clue also to the ideal of all art-creation. For no category will be adequate to the art-intelligence but that of unity, and no ideal but that of wholeness. And in the absolute sphere this ideal can be none other than the idea of absolute being itself. It is the idea of a nature in which unity is not reached through the compounding of differences, but in which the unity strikes first, so to speak, and differences arise through it and exist and are intelligible only in relation to it. The idea of absolute art is, therefore, absolute being conceived from the standpoint of its individual unity, that is, as a unity that comprehends all differences.

It is clear, in view of the above conceptions, that the art-process in the Absolute is identical with that of the absolute self-activity as a whole and in its most concrete form. This self-activity conceived in the light of the logos includes the categories of intellection or ideal truth and of volition or ideal good, as well as that of feeling or ideal beauty, and it enables us to reach the intuition of absolute art as realizing beauty, the ideal of feeling, under the highest idea or form of the intellect and in the mode of the ideal good, which is free self-expression.

Now, the idea of absolute art here reached does not differ materially from that of Plato, or his modern disciples, so far as they reproduce the spirit of the master. But in Plato's theory there are two defects. In the first place he does not anywhere clearly distinguish between absolute and relative art, and secondly, he is never able to hit upon a rational relation of the ideas of the beautiful and the good. He tends, therefore, continually to merge the beautiful in the good, and to restrict art to the representation of the good.

His shortcomings in this latter respect come out somewhat glaringly in his Republic, where for example, in adapting the products of art to pedagogical needs the Iliad is so expurgated as to metamorphose Homer into a species of Hellenic Tupper sedately aiming moral aphorisms at the heads of the Greeks. Had Plato carried out his dialectic more completely and realized the true distinction between the beautiful which is an emotional category, and the good which is a category of will, he would have been enabled to determine a sphere for art at once related to ethics and distinct from it.

Kant in all his Critiques has the vision of an intelligence that is constitutive, to use his own term, and whose activities are creative rather than representative. But he is never fully able to realize his intuition. It is clear, however, that in this notion of a constitutive intelligence is contained a germ which might be unfolded into the idea of self-activity, and it is clear also that the conception of such an activity would have supplied to Kant a clue he was constantly searching for but could never find, to the true idea of art.

Hegel has discovered this clue and conceives art to be the immediate self-manifestation of absolute spirit in the sensuous sphere, while the beautiful is the absolute idea shining in sensuous form. Hegel's intuition is the Platonic and he realizes clearly enough the essential nature of absolute beauty. But he falls into a difficulty analogous to that of Plato; namely, a failure to make a true distinction between the absolute and relative spheres and conceptions of art. In view of the modification which the absolute energy undergoes in constituting the categories of relativity it is evident that there can be no unmediated manifestation of the Absolute in sensuous form, and that the categories of relative art must be determined in view of this modification.

The sphere of absolute art is the absolute nature, and the objects of the absolute artist in that sphere is the eternal and absolute Spirit, which embodies the supernal beauty. Relative art-creation has two spheres, that of the creative artist and that of man. The relative products of the creative artist can be conceived only through a true idea of creation, which we have seen to be, not an immanental, but an outgoing, activity of the Absolute and to consist in the production of forms and energies of becoming in the sphere of non-being. We have also seen how the categories of the absolute energy are modified in this process into the categories of relativity, and how a process of development is grounded in which the creature passes from mechanism up to spirit.

It is only through the idea of creation as a mode of the absolute energy that a true notion of the work of the absolute artist in the sphere of becoming can be achieved. Creation is to be conceived as a formative energy working upon pure formless negation and producing out of it a relative, and not an absolute, manifestation. It is also through the same idea that an intelligible conception of the archetypes of becoming may be realized. We have already seen how the absolute energy becomes immanent in the world as the spiritual potentiality out of which its development springs. Here we have to add, that this potentiality is not undifferentiated capacity but rather a sphere of archetypal energies which realize themselves in the progressive categories of the world. This spiritual potential stands thus as the equivalent of the Aristotelian forms before they have become actualized. And conceived as containing the potential archetypes of the creation, this spiritual potence stands for the world-idea as it exists in the mind of the divine artist.

Now the world-idea as it embodies itself creatively in the spheres of cosmic and psychic nature, may be conceived as passing through the categories of mechanism, mechano-teleology, and teleology. Mechanism realizes itself in cosmic nature and has its norm in a mathematico-mechanical idea of order and harmony. The old Pythagorean notion of number as constituting the principle of cosmic order is an anticipation of this mechanical ideal. It is this notion of a mathematically complete order, harmony and system in space and time that must be conceived as constituting the immanent idea of art in the sphere of mechanical becoming. Mechano-teleology manifests itself in that process in cosmic nature which leads to its transcendence in the genesis of psychic nature. Its idea is that of mechanism as implicitly containing a teleologic principle which is wholly concealed in the inorganic sphere, but begins to manifest itself in the organic in the form of an explicit design or adaptation of organs and parts to a rational idea which can only be construed adequately as their end. In the sphere of organisms, therefore, we come upon the first explicit traces of teleology. It is only in the culmination of the organic, however, in the appearance of soul as an organ of spiritual self-activity that mechano-teleology reaches its climax, in the notion of the production of soul as the final goal of cosmic nature. In other words, it is only in psychic nature as embodied in man that the underlying design and rationality of cosmic nature is completely manifested.

Teleology is the artistic category of psychic nature. Here we enter the sphere of the explicit struggle of the ideal rational and spiritual, to overcome and transform the mechanical. The idea of this struggle and its solution is the immanent artistic motive of the psychic movement, while the transcendent ideal which stands as its goal is the idea of typal reconciliation between the psyche and its absolute ground. The artistic idea in the psychic sphere embraces therefore the whole struggle of humanity, viewed from the ideal teleologic standpoint, as a progressive triumph of the ideal rational and spiritual principle over its opposite, a triumph which realizes itself in sensuous, intellectual, moral, politico-social and religious stages. The supreme idea of art in the teleologic sphere is that of the absolute religion which embraces, as we have seen, a perfect form of mediation in its ideal synthesis of relative and absolute nature in the divine logos. Teleologically, the whole drama of becoming culminates in this idea.

The absolute artist thus realizes beauty in absolute and relative forms. Now, art creation viewed as a function of the human psyche, in the most general sense of the term, includes all civilization and culture, the whole output of humanity. But more restrictedly it embraces only that part of the output which has had for its dominating motive the gratification of what Mathew Arnold calls the sense for beauty. We have already analyzed the idea of beauty into the emotional apprehension of the unity of a whole, and the artistic intelligence into that free teleologic activity which proceeds from the idea of the whole to that of distinctions and details. It is activity working under the category of free self-expression rather than mechanical activity working under a law externally imposed. Now, an artistic product, even in its most rudimental form, whenever it is genuinely motived by the impulse of beauty, will be found to rise above the requirements of utilitarian necessity. Thus a drinking vessel will serve the utilitarian demand just as well if it is wholly devoid of beauty or even positively ugly. The motive that leads to the moulding of it into proportions of symmetry and to the executing on it of some design, however rude, of a vine or a drinking scene, will not, therefore, be the prompting of necessity, but will rather spring from the free impulse of beauty.

Art-creation then, as distinguished from other forms of human productivity, is free construction motived by the sense of beauty. This differentiates it from industry and all other forms of production. It is only the absolute Spirit, however, that can realize the ideal of absolute beauty. The psychic nature of man rises out of a dualism of being and non-being which determines its whole activity as a development from potence into actuality. The ideal of beauty, then, so far as it is realizable in a human intelligence, will be relative and imperfect. This being the case there will arise in the artistic sphere the same necessity for unending development as exists in other spheres of psychic activity. The perfect ideal is just as unattainable in art as it is in the spheres of morality and religion. Art aspires after the absolute beauty, but the ideal of its aims is something that can never be completely realized.

The soul of art is its creative spirit; its body is the mode of representation in which it manifests itself. This mode embraces both the principle and the form of representation. Plato originated the false theory that art is mere imitation, and he conceived imitation in the ignoble form of mimicry, thus confounding the first form of the art impulse with its essential nature. That the first form of the art impulse is imitation seems to be a well-established doctrine.* What is denied here is that the impulse would develop true art if it did not eventually rise above imitation. Aristotle adopts the Platonic idea, but represents imitation as something worthy and dignified. Now, there are branches of art, as statuary and portrait painting, in which imitation plays a leading part. But even here it is modified by the conception of the artist. Imitation is only a secondary principle in art proper, whose

* This follows from the general course of Psycho-genesis, which is from mechanism up to spirit. Genetically the art-impulse would first take the form of imitation. See an able and suggestive article on Imitation — A Chapter in the Natural History of Consciousness, by Professor J. Mark Baldwin, in *Mind*, January, 1894. The principle developed in this article would admit of a special application to the genesis of the art-impulse. Only we must here as elsewhere interpret the genetic process in the light of the basal category of spirit which is development from mechanism to self-activity. Imitation is the mechanical moment in a process through which it is at length subordinated to a higher form of activity.

essence is free creation. Art does not imitate life merely, but reproduces it with a free hand and embodies it in its characteristic forms. The form of art-representation is both *sensuous* and *symbolic*. In its sensuous form it appeals to either eye or ear and expresses itself either in the static order of coexistence in space or in the dynamic order of the time-series. As symbolic the static branch subdivides into the plastic and the pictorial, the former employing as its material, substances that are capable of being moulded into solid form, the latter achieving its results by means of a blending of color and light and shade on a flat surface. The dynamic branch employs the rhythmic series of sound and subdivides according as the sounds are simply tones or articulate speech. We thus arrive at the following classification according to sensuous and symbolic form. (1) *Static :* architecture, sculpture, and painting. (2) *Dynamic :* music, poetry and artistic prose.

Art may also be classified according to the degree in which it realizes freedom of expression, as follows :—architecture, which is hampered both by utility and mass ; sculpture, which escapes utility and reduces mass ; painting, which escapes mass, and is limited only by the capacity of light and colors to create perspective ; poetry and artistic prose, which escape spatial restrictions and are bound only by the limits of rhythmic succession of articulate sounds, and lastly music, which escapes the restrictions of articulate speech and is obliged to observe only one limit, that of rhythmic tone. In the freedom of its expression music is, therefore, the supreme art, since its rhythmic forms present, so to speak, typal moulds into which infinite varieties of spiritual histories may be poured.

The question as to relative worth and dignity of modes of representation arises in the sphere of each art, but has no special significance as between diffent types of art. Every art may be made a vehicle of the highest spiritual expression, and all arts are, therefore, equally worthy in themselves. Different arts may, however, and do, differ in their capacities for various modes of representation. Thus an important distinction between the static and dynamic arts consists in the superior capacity of the former to express more and to express it more completely, in the unity of a single representation. Sculpture, painting, and architecture are in this respect vastly superior to music and literature. On the other hand, the dynamic arts have a great advantage in their superior capacity for representing the stages of spiritual history. While, therefore, in their power to gather up a history into a single representation, they are greatly inferior to the static arts, they are perhaps more than compensated for this by their capacity for a series of representations in which almost unbounded liberty as to details is enjoyed. One of Lessing's greatest contributions to the philosophy of art is his recognition of this distinction. Lessing also observes the other fact which is a deduction from the primal distinction; namely, the greater freedom of expression which is enjoyed by the dynamic arts. All art is free to represent the ugly and the horrible as well as the beautiful, provided that in the whole representation these features be subordinated to the requirements of beauty. But, as Lessing shows in his reflections on the *Laocoon*, this proviso is a much more stringent limit upon freedom in the static than in the dynamic arts. And the stringency is only partially relieved in a series of representations which embody a history. But in the dynamic arts, where it is not the repose of the figures or the perfection of single pulsations, but the progressive movement, that impresses, there may be included an indefinite amount of horrible and repulsive details, provided the movement as a whole realizes the idea of the beautiful.

On the whole, it is doubtless true that the greater freedom of musical and literary representation renders these arts superior as vehicles of spiritual self-expression. There seems to be a philosophical reason for this at once profound and simple. The inner motive of art-creation, as we have seen, is what may be called a sense for wholeness. Now, the conception of this sense for wholeness as operating under the category of free self-expression, gives us the most general idea of love. Love seeks wholeness and love is, therefore, everywhere synthetic and mediatory. But mediation is, as we have seen, not only the inner core of all relative spiritual history, but it is a teleologic idea which can be realized only in a dynamic series. The representation-form of music and literature is this dynamic series, and this renders them the most fitting vehicles for the representation of the drama of mediation.

The greatest and most typal spiritual theme of art is a struggle which is mediated by love and ends in reconciliation and peace. Music, on account of its freedom from the definite suggestiveness of articulate speech, is the highest vehicle of this mediational motive and touches most profoundly the fountains of love. Literature in its supremest forms of epic and dramatic poetry, is an embodiment of this same typal spiritual theme. The epic works out the struggle and achieves its mediation and unity in the broad field of national or tribal history, while the drama embodies the same theme in the sphere of particular individualities. Comedy presents the lighter phases of the theme, while in tragedy the deepest notes of spiritual experience are struck. The struggle is to the death and mediation can be achieved only by the shedding of blood, while the reconciliation and peace which ensues is the attainment of a higher plane of spiritual life and experience. Aristotle has a profound insight into the cathartic quality of real tragedy which renders it a means of purification through terror and pity. A profounder and simpler insight will see in it, as its core of spiritual meaning, a drama of love and mediation.

Art and religion are very closely allied both in

their history and their essence. It is in the common theme of the highest music and the profoundest literature that their ideas seem to coalesce. In the same theme we seem to discover the inner spiritual idea of art in the light of which the whole development becomes teleologic. For just as the real teleology of cosmic nature manifests itself in soul, and the real teleology of psychic nature reveals itself in the perfect type of religion, so here in the idea of spiritual struggle mediated through sacrifice, and reconciliation and peace achieved on a higher plane, we seem to find the real teleologic ideal of art.

Art-appreciation is not a category of the artist, but rather of the spectator and student of art. This appreciation has two branches, the intellectual and the emotional, and it passes through psychological and ontological stages. Ontologically its intellectual branch is a species of rational knowledge and consists in the apprehension of the fundamental ideas of art. Rational art-knowledge, in common with other forms, can be completely achieved only in the light of the categories of being, non-being, and becoming. For the philosophy of art, in common with all philosophy, must find its starting-point in the idea of absolute being. From this idea it is able to deduce the notions of absolute creativeness and absolute beauty. But these ideas cannot, as we have seen, be carried over unmodified into the relative sphere. We cannot truly define human art as the Absolute manifesting itself in sensuous form until by a true conception of non-being and the dualistic conditions of creation, we have achieved a rational idea of the form of becoming and its differentia. It will then be possible to conceive the presence and activity of a principle of absolute intelligence in the psychic sphere, producing manifestations that do not transcend the relative limitations. This is a crucial point in art as it is in all philosophic theory. The psychic intelligence contains an absolute principle. But this principle is embodied in a dualistic and developing type of individuality, and this difference of type determines its actual consciousness as relative and distinguished from the Absolute. Art, so far as it is a function of the human psyche, is a manifestation of the dual psychic activity in sensuous form.

Psychologic art-appreciation on its intellectual side manifests itself as art-perception. It follows an empirical and genetic order, beginning with the simplest and most sensuous relations whose apprehensions are accompanied with pleasurable or painful feeling, and passing through stages corresponding pretty well to those laid down to Socrates by the Theban prophetess. In its path upward the psyche first apprehends the beauty of sensuous forms in colors and physical proportions. A higher stage is the apprehension of the mathematical relations of symmetry, harmony, and proportion. The upward footsteps then enter the sphere of teleology, passing through the portal of mechano-teleology into teleology proper, where the spiritual types of beauty are realized, its highest manifestation being in the ideal form of spiritual mediation and unity embodied in the highest conceptions of art and religion.

Art-appreciation on the side of feeling is the emotional impulse aroused by the contemplation of the beautiful. It is the *Eros* of the Greeks and expresses not simply passive enjoyment, but an active appropriation of the object. The art-feeling, like other forms of spiritual activity, however, passes from a potential stage of relative passivity to one of realized actuality. It begins as a feeling of pleasure or pain that is immediately aroused by the contemplation of sensuous beauty. The development of actuality in the æsthetic emotion accompanies the progress of the ideal element. As the higher ideas and relations of beauty dawn upon the intelligence they constitute the ideal basis of higher forms of æsthetic emotion. Thus the emotional appreciation of the beautiful rises through the categories of moral beauty to that of spiritual beauty proper, the sphere of the religious emotions, and culminates in the ecstatic state of emotion aroused by the beauty of holiness.

Art and utility are very closely related in certain departments of art, as for example in architecture. But even here art begins where utility leaves off. A homely and even hideous structure will serve the ends of utilitarian comfort. It is the sense for beauty that dictates and motives all the features of architecture that can be called artistic. This is universally true and the only claim utility can have on beauty is that of self-preservation. It can justly demand that it be not sacrificed in the interest of beauty.

Art and morality are more intimately connected. They are one in the sense that the supreme motive of both is love, and so far as morality embodies love, it is beautiful. The relation of the moral law to art, however, is analogous to that of utility. Morality has the right to demand that its law be respected and that the good be not sacrificed in the interest of beauty.

The relations between art and religion are of the closest kind. The form of the artistic intelligence is the same as that of religion. Both are synthetic and teleologic, operating under the categories of unity and design. Both are spiritual and concrete, appealing with equal power to reason and feeling. And both contemplate in their highest forms the same spiritual ideal, the solution of spiritual struggle and the realization of unity and peace on a higher plane through mediational sacrifice.

XV

KNOWLEDGE

Knowledge is not reality, but the conception of reality. The real is, therefore, its presupposition. To deny reality is to abolish the possibility of knowledge. But the denial is not dangerous, for it begins with the denial of itself. If the sphere of knowledge is only a sphere of illusion, then illusion itself becomes real. Illusion is not an ultimate concept. It is the real masquerading in a false dress. The false dress presupposes normal clothing. The illusory is a species within the genus real.

Regarding knowledge, four fundamental questions arise: (1) How is knowledge possible? (2) How is it made actual? (3) How are the processes of knowledge correlated? (4) Has knowledge any limit?

The first question involves two considerations: (1) the presupposition; (2) the first principle of knowledge. McCosh says the presupposition of knowledge is reality, and this we also assert. If the real is not, then knowledge falls into self-contradiction. To say, however, that knowledge presupposes the real is only affirming in other words that philosophy must have a primal datum to start from. A little reflection will show the identity of these propositions. The reality assumed cannot be every or any sort of existence. Let us start with some phenomenon which is a species of reality and we find ourselves forced back of the phenomenon to its antecedent in time. But the temporal antecedent is only a passing stage in a procession of reason which moves on from the idea of antecedent to that of causal nexus as a form of mechanical activity and from this to the idea of ground or activity that returns upon itself and is, therefore, self-existent. This proves that every assumption is provisional except the last, and that every species of reality except the last is provisionally assumed and depends upon that last for its justification.

The unconditional assumption of knowledge, that on which all provisional assumptions depend, is absolute reality. We thus come back to the primal insight of Plato and Aristotle, who saw that philosophy must have an absolute foundation. This absolute was construed by Aristotle, as we already know, into *purus actus*, or pure self-activity, in which there is no unrealized potency. The conclusion we reach here is simply a reassertion of the Aristotelian principle which makes absolute reality, that is, absolute self-activity, the first and only unconditional presupposition of knowledge.

This first presupposition of knowledge leads us by a few steps to the first principle of knowledge. When Descartes pointed to self-consciousness as the first principle of philosophy and defined mind as thinking substance, he had one foot in the kingdom but was misled by his false notion of substance. Had he learned the lesson of Aristotle and translated the idea of substance into that of self-activity, his whole theory would have been revolutionized. If to the position here asserted, that pure self-activity is the first presupposition of knowledge, we add the position reached in the chapter on Consciousness; namely, that self-activity and self-conscious activity are identical, we arrive at the idea of *self-consciousness as the first principle of knowledge.* But so conceived it is a more effective principle than that of Descartes. For the idea of substance has been translated into the idea of self-activity, and when self-consciousness and self-conscious activity are identified the principle of self-consciousness becomes one with the principle of self-activity. Self-consciousness thus absorbs the idea of substance into itself.

The consequences of this are far-reaching. In the first place it reveals the fact that all knowledge rests on an absolute first principle. If the presupposition of knowledge is pure self-activity, and its first principle self-consciousness, which is conscious self-activity, then it is clear that no categories short of pure self-activity and the consciousness of pure self-activity will serve as primal grounds for knowledge. But pure self-activity is absolute being and pure self-consciousness is the self-consciousness of absolute being. The ground and first principle of knowledge are, therefore, absolute.

Descartes apprehended, though not very clearly, the force of this reflection when he argued that the existence of an infinite and perfect being is the necessary presupposition of the self-consciousness of man, a contention that is perfectly sound, but which rests on its true and irrefragable ground only when the principle in the human consciousness is asserted to be absolute in its essence and, therefore, in its perfect activity, the necessary bearer of an absolute consciousness. Absolute being is thus an immediate presupposition of self-consciousness.

In the second place, this conception of self-consciousness enables us to discover and ground the categories of an adequate and comprehensive theory of knowledge. Self-activity is the immediate presupposition of self-consciousness, but its primal categories are those of self and the not-self conceived as its negative opposite. That both these categories are not categories of being will appear from the following reflection. Absolute being is pure self-activity, and pure self-consciousness is consciousness of pure self-activity. The self then of the dual categories must be self-active. What then is the not-self? What is it that can be distinguished from self-activity as its negation? There is no completely rational answer to this possible, except one that endows being with a primal power to distinguish itself from its negative opposite, non-being. And this non-being cannot, therefore, be conceived as in being but as out of it, as its qualitative opposite and adversary.

The primal not-self, or object, of pure self-activity or absolute being is not, then, anything internal to being. It is not being (self-activity) going out in self-alienation into its other, for this other would still be the self and the dialectic which leads to it would be only the activity of internal self-evolution. The primal not-self is the negative and foe of all this self-active process. It is something that must be annuled before the universe can contain any other conscious individualities distinct from the self-conscious absolute. How this negative of being is to be conceived and characterized, we have treated at length in the chapter on Being and Non-Being. The point we wish to insist on here is that the primal categories of reality are being and non-being, and that non-being is not the *alter ego* but the opposite of being. The *alter ego* of being is being in some form, but the negative of being is its opposite, non-being.

Now, it is to be remembered that while these categories of self and not-self are primal in self-consciousness, there is an immediate presupposition of self-consciousness and that is self-activity. If we call this being, we may then say that the very first step of all is being's consciousness of self. Being becomes conscious of itself. This is the principle of self-consciousness. The second step is that of the distinction noted above. Being becomes conscious of itself as distinguished from and opposed to non-being; that is, negation and want. The fact that self-consciousness is the presupposition of this distinction between self and not-self, has led some thinkers to the conclusion that self-consciousness is the unity of self and its negative, or as they prefer to say, subject and object. The logic of this position is that the negative is only the other of the self and ultimately identical with it. Self-consciousness is thus made a one-sided principle of comprehension which identifies opposites, and comprehends in being want and negation as well as the plenum of positive reality. But it must be evident that if this absolute principle comprehends vacuum, that is, want and negation, its integrity and its absoluteness are destroyed. The Absolute as pure self-activity must exclude want, negation, and imperfection.

We must construe the principle of self-consciousness as the unity of being and as the principle which, therefore, distinguishes being from its not-self, negation and want, and excludes it as qualitatively outside of and opposed to it. The primal category of knowledge, after its first principle, self-consciousness, is the distinction of self from its negative, or as we prefer to say, being from non-being. Now, knowledge we have defined as the conception or idea of reality. The two terms of reality here reached are being and non-being. A complete theory of knowledge must then embrace conceptions of non-being as well as conceptions of being. We have seen, however, in the second and third chapters of this book, that no positive idea of non-being is possible. Non-being is the purely negative term in the universe of reality. As pure negative it must be represented by negative conceptions. We have seen that it may be best symbolized as an outer sphere which contains the negative opposites of the energies of being, and which must, therefore, be overcome in order that being may realize itself.

The part which non-being plays as a datum in a theory of knowledge enters in those modifications of relativity which cannot otherwise be explained. Postulating the negative, however, it may be said that the chief industry of a theory of knowledge is to be devoted to the discovery and exposition of the categories of being. In fact its sole interest consists in tracing the fortunes of being, non-being playing the part of an adversary that must be warred against and overcome.

Those thinkers who adopt the monal concept of reality criticised above, also limit the inner dialectic of being to self-affirmation and self-negation. But the conception of non-being as the antithetic of being cancels the moment of self-negation and makes it necessary to distinguish between the internal activity of self-affirmation and the transitive energy by which being goes out upon its opposite. We have seen in the chapters on Being and Non-being, and Becoming, how non-being supplies a rational motive for this outgo of energy and thus grounds negatively the whole process of becoming. It is this dual energizing of self-assertion, and negation of the not-self or non-being, that is comprehended in the unity of self-consciousness. The dual activity is a function of being, therefore, but the negated is not included, but excluded and opposed by the energy of being. The idea of the self-negation of being involves a subtle self-contradiction.

The dialectic of self-consciousness begins with the primal distinction between self and not-self. The not-self is non-being, the negation and opposite of the self. The second step is one in which the self is volitionally asserted, and the not-self volitionally denied. But this denial of the not-self is not a pure intellectual activity of the self; it is rather its volitional activity which is to be construed as the putting forth of creative energy in the process of producing being out of non-being.

Of this compound dialectic the first step is dominantly a process of intellection. In the logic of being conception precedes and is presupposed in volition. Else the whole movement is dark and irrational. The position of Schopenhauer and his school is an inversion of the necessary logic of being. But they draw the inevitable conclusion from their transposed premises. If we invert the world it becomes irrational and absurd, and life becomes a ghastly joke. We agree with the philosophy that identifies the Absolute with absolute thought, in its main contention; namely, that logically the first activity of all must be intellection. The Absolute must *think* in order to *will* and *act* rationally. We only deprecate in such thinking its rationalistic tendency to force every spiritual function into the intellectual mould, a tendency which may be cured by the reflection that in the Absolute, which can only be conceived as pure actuality without undeveloped potence, there may be logical dependence, but no derivation. If we do not mean then to eliminate volitional function from our idea of the Absolute, we must conceive its dependence on intellection in a way that will consist with its originality. This, we think, is possible only on the supposition that self-conscious activity has three perfectly primal and inseparable modes or aspects; that in one aspect it is intellection; in another emotion; in another volition; but that in every movement of its activity, intellection is the first presupposition.

If in this sense the *first* act of the spiritual dialectic is one of thinking, we can see how the intellectual activity completes its circle, going out from itself in the intuition of the negative outer sphere and returning upon itself enriched with a dual intuition of being and non-being. And this will motive, as we have seen, the *second* act, which is one of will, the volitional activity going out in the energy of creation into the negative sphere, and returning upon itself enriched with a dual realization of being and becoming, or, in other phrase, of self and the other. This again, to complete the movement, will motive the *third* act, which is dominantly one of unity, in which the absolute activity, going out in the energy of love upon the other, or becoming, returns upon itself enriched with a dual realization of self and the other reconciled.

In this dialectic of spiritual activity it is fundamental to observe that the primal intellectual intuition which differentiates non-being from being is not mediated, but stands open, and that this supplies the motive for the whole consequent dialectic, the will to cancel the negative by producing being in its sphere, which gives rise to the creature, a nature that contains the potentiality of spiritual being, and lastly the outflow of synthetic love which mediates the spiritual evolution of the creature and brings it into harmony with the creative spirit. A clear conception of this, as we think, fundamental truth, will make it plain that non-being cannot be comprehended as a moment in the evolution of being, but that it is the opposite of spirit and to be mediated only by being overcome. This mediation can be effected only by volition and love, and has for its moments creation and evolution, the production of potential being out of non-being and the development of this potence toward the ideal of actualized spirit.

In grounding a theory of knowledge it is not customary to go so deep into ontology. The sufficient justification for doing so, however, is its necessity. The first principle of knowledge is self-consciousness, and we have seen that this cannot be conceived in any other way than as conscious self-activity. It, therefore, absorbs the idea of substance into it and becomes also the first principle of ontology. It is impossible to develop a rational theory of knowledge without showing the ontologic grounds on which it rests, and since a complete theory of knowledge must include both the Absolute and the relative, its structural ontology will include a rational insight into the nature of absolute and relative being. Not only so, but since there is a difference between absolute and relative as well as a sameness, these relations must have their reason for knowledge in real ontological grounds. For it is rationally clear that no theory of knowledge can profess adequacy which does not correlate the world and its absolute ground in such a manner that reflection may find in the ground the rationale, not only of the world's existence, but also of its distinctive nature and evolution.

From the development of the first principle of knowledge and the presupposition of reality on which it rests, namely, that of self-existence, we reach a structural conception of the system of reality. And this, taken as a whole, is to be regarded as the condition of the possibility of knowledge. For, when the situation has been thoroughly analyzed, the discovery is made that the real presupposition of knowledge is a whole system of reality; that the assumption of self-existence leads reflection by an inevitable route to the ideas of being and non-being and the sphere of dependent being and relativity. Knowledge confronts this structural system of things and its practical problem is how this system of reality is to be actualized in the consciousness of the individual. This ranks as the second great question in a theory of knowledge.

The mode of individual acquisition is grounded in the nature of the human soul. The soul, as we have seen, is a developing spiritual principle. It is, therefore, dual in its constitution, combining in itself both potence and actuality. As a developing potence it is a flowing stream; as an actuality it is a self-centred individual. Its life and evolution consist in a progressive dialectic between these terms, in which the tendency is to pass from a stage in which the life is dominated by mechanical categories to one in which spirit has realized its free activity. This idea of the soul as a developing spiritual principle explains two fundamental characteristics of individual knowledge. The first is the possibility of knowledge being an individual possession at all when its first principle is a universal. There is a common fund of reality, but there can be no common fund of knowledge. This arises from the fact that man is a developing creature. If he were absolute there would be a common fund of knowledge, but there would be only one being to enjoy it, for there can be but one absolute consciousness. But, as we have seen in the preceding chapter, the mode of man's spiritual activity as a developing creature, determines his conscious individuality and will as distinct. The human consciousness, therefore, contains an absolute principle; namely, that of spiritual self-activity, but in man, it is a principle of a developing life that is ever passing through potence to actuality in the stages of growth and evolution.

The second fundamental characteristic of knowledge which the idea of the soul explains is the process of acquisition. From mechanism to spirit is the law of evolution. The process of acquisition will follow this law, and the stages in the development of its modes, from sensation up to the highest rational activity, will correspond to and depend on the stages in the evolution of the spiritual principle. The fact that in the beginnings of the intellectual activity the categories of space and time determine the form of experience, is not wholly explained by conceiving a budding soul in a bodily organism; but a deeper root of this is to be found in the fact that the spiritual potence of the soul is itself in that stage of activity when the form of its activity is most dominated by the mechanical categories. This explains why the whole representation-framework of its life is mechanical, so that any truth that aims to reach the inner citadel of apprehension must come thickly coated in the dress of material representation.

As the life progresses the modes of apprehension change; the merely spatio-temporal forms begin to give place to the dynamic, and the intelligence begins to grasp causation, the inner principle of the series. This marks the starting-point of reflection and of the intellectual life proper. For the apprehension of causation, even in its most mechanical form, leads the mind to look from the fact to the condition out of which it rises. And this marks the transition from mere representation to conception, which is the first term of the life of reflection. The central principle of the conceptive form of intellection is causation conceived as a bond that connects phenomena with a chain or series of conditions. It is the dominating category of that middle stage of mentality to which the name understanding has been applied. But the evolution of spiritual activity makes it impossible for the reflective life to stop here. Mechanical causation which holds phenomena in the bonds of conditions external to them is not an ultimate form of activity, but has coiled up in it the suggestion of a mode of activity that transcends it. In other words reflection must progress from the idea of the dependent, or that which has the reason of its being outside of itself, to the idea of ground, or that which has the reason of its being within itself and is, therefore, self-existent. The idea of ground is that of self-activity, and thus in the notion of ground spirit has achieved an idea of its own highest category which is self-explanatory.

Thus the intellectual life culminates on the objective side in the category of self-existence or absolute being which we have seen in another connection to be the unconditional presupposition of knowledge. On its inner side the conscious life passes from its representation-form, in which flows the life of the purely empirical self, through the concept-form, which embodies the empirico-rational self, up to the idea-form, whose principle is self-consciousness and whose embodiment is the purely rational self. On its inner side, therefore, the intellectual life culminates in the principle of self-consciousness, which we have found to be the ground-principle of knowledge. By following the clew furnished by the idea of a spiritual principle developing from potence to actuality, we are thus able to show how the process of acquisition leads up to that synthesis of ground-principle and presupposition on which the possibility of knowledge depends.

The third fundamental question is that of the correlation of processes of knowledge. There are two generic methods, the deductive or rational, and the inductive or empirical. These are both founded on what are called the fundamental axioms of thought; namely, identity and contradiction, or, in Platonic phrase, the same and the different, and sufficient reason. Now, these laws when reduced to their primal form resolve into the dialectic of spirit which we have already unfolded. This dialectic is a primal antithetic of thinking by which self-including being excludes its opposite, non-being.

The two antithetic categories, the same and the different, constitute the primeval eyes of thinking, and its original constitution, therefore, predetermines it to be ever on the search for the same throughout a chaos of differences. Translating this into terms of self-activity which is the highest category of spirit, we may say that the fundamental law of thinking is dual, and that it is of the essence of thought to think itself inclusively, and its opposite exclusively and antithetically. This dialectic functions at the heart of all intellectual processes. But it is capable of two different modes of application, and these modes are the two generic methods. If we start with a rational presupposition and apply our dual dialectic to it, the method is rational. Here the thought is a two-armed instrument and the movement of demonstration is the self-inclusion of the same and the antithetic exclusion of the different. Thought thus cuts both ways, like a double ploughshare, and the demonstrated result of the process is the thought's own self-included offspring. The hackneyed syllogism, "Man is mortal, Socrates is a man; therefore, Socrates is mortal," illustrates this. The thought has combined humanity and mortality, and wherever it finds humanity it reasserts itself and binds humanity to its fellow, mortality. But this process of inclusion is by itself an abstraction and impossible. The act that connects man and mortality is only half a complete thought. The concrete thought has its negative exclusive side, not-mortal, not-man, which forms the negative background of the intellection and follows it through every step to the end. The dialectic of thought is negative and exclusive as well as positive and inclusive. But it never negates or excludes itself, always its opposite.

If, however, we start, not with a rational presupposition but a fact or group of facts, the same dialectic will proceed in a different manner. In the rational process the dialectic proceeds from an assumed relation, and its business is that of dual inclusion and exclusion under this relation. But here we seem to have isolated facts without any relation. Thought, however, cannot get on without relations.

How then does the dialectic of thought apply to the case? Evidently in this way: In thinking, reason includes her own, but excludes and negates her opposite. Now, facts without relations, that is, isolated unaccounted facts, are irrational. Thought expels them from her province and then goes out upon them by a volitional act in order to overcome them and create a rational system out of the irrational. Here we get at the root of the other great principle of thinking; namely, sufficient reason. For sufficient reason is not a purely intellectual principle, but contains an element of volition. It is the demand of the human spirit that the irrational shall be suppressed, and that out of it shall be produced a rational system. This demand, which arises in view of the negative, is the motive that leads to the reference of isolated facts or groups to their causal conditions. The result is the emergence of a rational order out of the irrational. And we have only to follow this process through its successive stages of rational genesis until it reaches the highest category and realizes a spiritual result, in order to see that in this law of sufficient reason we have struck a motive, in substance the same as that which we have been led to attribute to the absolute spirit as the motive of creation.

Now, regarding the correlation of these two processes, rational and empirical, it is clear that they ought to mutually bear out and supplement one another. For whether we start with a rational supposition and come down to the details of its application under the guidance of the dual law of identity and difference, or begin with irrational and isolated facts, or groups, and proceed upward under the impulse of sufficient reason, we are but traversing the same circle in opposite directions, and ought to come around to some point where the conclusion of one method will bear out the other. That this is the true idea of correlation finds confirmation in the fact illustrated in the first division of this chapter; namely, that if we start from self-consciousness as the first principle of knowledge, we are led by rational reflection upon it to a structural ontology in which a sphere of relative and created being is grounded on the self-existent absolute. Whereas, if we start from phenomena and follow the demand of sufficient reason, we are led step by step to a point where we find in self-existence the objective ground, and in self-consciousness the inner principle of all rational knowledge. The result here is, on the one hand, the grounding of the empirical sphere by means of the rational method; on the other, the confirmation of the primal data of the rational method by means of the empirical procedure.

That one method should confirm the other is only rational. For whether we start with the principle of identity and difference, or with that of sufficient reason, the procedure is one and the same, the self-assertion of spirit against its negative. If we proceed upon the former principle, spirit asserts itself overtly and explicitly, and excludes and sublates its negative; whereas, if our procedure is under the principle of sufficient reason, spirit overtly and explicitly excludes and sublates the negative, while the implicit motive of its whole movement is its assertion of itself. The whole movement, for instance, of the logic of Hegel is intelligible and rational if we conceive that here spirit is proceeding under the principle of sufficient reason and asserting itself against the negative in an activity which is continually producing out of the irrational the stages of a rational evolution. On the other hand, Hegel's ordinary procedure is an application of identity and difference, the principle of the common logic, and its dialectic when truly understood consists in an overt dualistic movement in which spirit persistently asserts and includes itself, while it just as persistently excludes and sublates its negative.

As to the limits of knowledge, we have seen that all method is reducible to one formula, spirit's assertion of itself. Now, as spirit includes both absolute and relative, this formula must include the whole continent of reality. Logically, then, there can be no *à priori* limit of knowledge. The principle of knowledge is all-comprehensive, and this renders omniscience logically possible. But there is an ontological, or rather an onto-psychological, principle of limitation which is to be found in the nature of the human soul. We have seen that the soul is not pure actuality, but rather a spiritual principle that is passing continually from potence to actuality. This means that the soul is an imperfect, developing creature. Now, undeveloped potence is, as we have seen, a limitation which determines the distinctive form and bounds of the soul's activity. It is here that we strike the true limit of knowledge. It is a limit of energy, of spirit's power of asserting itself, and rests therefore primarily in the will, and not in the thought or intelligence.

The limit of knowledge is, therefore, not fixed but movable. As the human spirit unfolds into actuality, its power of asserting itself increases, and as its intelligence unfolds, thought in its self-assertion is able to master progressively higher categories. The highest category is that of spirit itself, and when the human soul is able to realize all things completely under the self-active category of spirit, it is able to say that it apprehends even as it is apprehended.

XVI

LOGOS

We have seen in the first chapter of this book that the logos-principle is the norm of intelligibility in the sphere of reality. What this logos-principle is we are now able more clearly to determine. Historically, the principle has its ontologic root in the idealism of Plato. From Plato it gradually worked its way into the heart of philosophic thinking until, under the spiritual impulse of Christianity, it became, as the category of immanent self-conscious personality, the constructive norm of theological as well as philosophical conceptions. The unapproachable One of Neo-Platonism, the unrelated Absolute of Hellenic Judaism, which is connected with the world only through an external logos, becomes the divine logos, the Being who is internally self-conscious and personal and who manifests himself as the Creator of the world out of non-being, and as the mediator who leads the world out of its alienation up to God. Psychologically, we have found this same principle energizing at the centre of modern thinking as the basis of certitude and the ground-category of knowledge. In modern philosophy it is the principle of self-consciousness, which, as conceived by Descartes failed to realize its full power. But the tendency of modern thinking has been in the direction of a species of psychological immanence which conceives the logos as the inner category of substance and thus translates it into living spirit.

The principle of self-consciousness becomes thus a norm of conscious self-activity, and conscious self-activity is identical with personal, spiritual being. And combining the ontologic and psychologic intuitions, the conclusion is reached that all being is in its core spiritual and personal.

It is clear, then, that the logos-principle and the principle of pure self-conscious personality are identical; that when we call God the logos, we call him the self-conscious personal being, and that when we call man a self-conscious personal being we thereby conceive him as a being of whose spiritual nature the logos is the immanent principle. There is then a relation of sameness between the absolute spirit and the soul of man in the principle which determines their conscious and personal life.

This vital point gives rise to two important considerations. The first concerns the function of the logos-principle as enabling us to determine the inner natures, respectively, of the absolute spirit and the soul of man. Regarding absolute spirit, we only need here to summarize the results of former reflections. In the chapter on Knowledge we were able, by conceiving the logos-principle as a norm of spiritual activity, to follow the immanent dialectic of spirit and determine the self-conscious personal life of the Absolute under three logically correlated aspects, as absolute thought, absolute will, and absolute love. And by construing the negative side of this dialectic in the light of the same principle we were able to see how the intuition of non-being arising in the primal activity of absolute thought, supplies the motive for the out-go of the absolute will in the creation of the world in the sphere of non-being, and how also the imperfect and undeveloped nature of the creature, its distance from the creator, supplies the motive for the out-go of the absolute love in the work of evolution and mediation.

The principle is equally potent in revealing the inner nature of the human soul. We have seen how the true idea of the creative function leads to a rational conception of becoming and relative nature. It determines the soul as a spiritual potence which is consciously passing into actuality, as a developing creature, therefore, with an infinite spiritual ideal. It leads, therefore, to a rational conception of the dualism of the soul's conscious experience, and enables us to translate it into a struggle of the ideal principle of self-conscious activity, to overcome and comprehend the flowing stream of the empirical life. And it further leads to a rational idea of the conscious stages which the soul passes through in this dual evolution. For just as the application of the idea of self-conscious dialectic enables us to conceive three logically correlated aspects of the personal life of the Absolute; namely, absolute thought, absolute will, and absolute love; so in the psychic sphere its application reveals to us a corresponding dialectic in which the spirit asserts itself intellectually in the principle of identity and difference, volitionally in the principle of sufficient reason and æsthetically in the principle of unity which is the soul of love. But in the human spirit this self-assertion is an ideal that is never completely realized, since the spirit itself is a developing potence whose basal movement is an evolution.

The second consideration is that of the relation between the absolute logos and the spirit of man. We have seen that in the possession of a common principle they are the same. But this sameness is only community of essence. It justifies the assertion, that the ideal principle of man's spiritual nature is absolute, and that he may, therefore, be the bearer of absolute ideas and a knowledge of the Absolute. But this only implies community of essence. The modification which constitutes man a creature; namely, the form of his spiritual activity as a growth or evolution from potence to actuality, which also determines the order of his progress from mechanism to spirit, is the basis of his distinction of consciousness, individuality, and will. This constitutes him the bearer of a conscious life whose principle is ideally absolute, but whose individuality is relative and distinct.

There is thus community and distinction between the absolute logos and the spirit of man. And we have seen in the chapter on Religion how, through this community of spiritual principle embodying itself on the one hand in the soul's ideal and on the other in the Divine logos, a medium of interaction and intercommunion is maintained between the soul and its transcendent ground.

The logos stands thus as a fruitful norm of philosophic ideas. It is the principle from which a rational conception of absolute being may be deduced. Without it only the existence of an absolute could be affirmed, while its nature would baffle conception. It is the only principle also that makes a true conception of the dualistic dialectic of spirit possible. Without the insight it gives the true nature and differentia of relativity would be hidden mysteries, and no adequate conception of the nature of the human spirit and its relation to the Absolute would be possible. On any other principle agnosticism could not be clearly transcended, nor yet pantheism or atheistic individualism. The logos is a principle that intelligizes the whole system of reality, binding absolute and relative each to each in close bonds, without infringing the vested rights of either.

The logos also mediates the evolution of the world-process. The categories of its progress are, as we have seen, mechanism, life, and spirit. The mechanical forces are the first actualities of the potential world-ground. They act without consciousness or teleologic motive of their own, but they are not to be conceived, therefore, as blindly working forces, for hidden in them is the will of the logos working under the category unity. Cosmic nature is the sphere of mechanism and of mechanical forces and laws. But her presupposition is a spiritual activity which can alone supply a completely rational idea of her order.

The world-process, under the impelling will of the logos at length transcends the pure mechanical stage and enters that of life, where the spiritual principle begins to function as an immanent unifying force in the production of organisms. In the plant consciousness is transcendent, but it enters the animal as instinct and feeling, and the animal is able, therefore, to assert itself against a merely mechanical existence and to develop a species of imperfect individuality. But to the animal, ideality is still a hidden force. The animal is a blind servant of the logos and represents only a transitional stage in the passage of the world from the cosmic to the psychic sphere.

The category of life is that of mechano-teleology. Its overt forces and laws are mechanical, but under the influence of the hidden activity of the logos these forces realize a product which transcends them and points necessarily to a spiritual ground. In the psychic nature, as we have seen, the logos becomes immanent as a principle of self-conscious activity and experience, not as the logos of God, however, bringing with it an absolute consciousness, but rather as the ideal principle in the consciousness of an imperfect and developing creature. Here it functions as the principle of knowledge and as the organ that contains the ideal norms of philosophy, science, morality, and art.

It is by virtue of the logos-principle also that the soul of man is able to transcend the limits of its particular individuality and to achieve a race-consciousness as the arena for a historic experience and common civic life. Here its output is culture and civilization and all that splendid and pathetic record that is embodied in human history. In this sphere the logos also functions as a principle of spiritual freedom motiving and inspiring that teleologic upward movement of social, intellectual, and spiritual progress, which through and over all negative opposition and in spite of all subversive and destructive tendencies has made the historic record, with all its obverse side of darkness and disorder, one of splendid and enduring achievement.

But not without the Logos of God. The deepest intuition of philosophy is that which beholds the spirit of man in close and living union with its divine fellow. The human psyche is never away from the logos of God, but, as the profound Descartes asserted, the conscious principle which gives the soul its idea of self gives it also in inseparable fellowship its idea of God. The plummet that sounds the profoundest depths of psychic nature touches also the nature of God. That God and the psyche are identical is, and ever must be, precluded by the basal type of psychic nature. But there is unity of principle in diversity of type and distinction of consciousness. The psychic logos and the logos of God are one in their ground principle. Only, the latter is *purus actus* in the nature and consciousness of the Absolute, while the psychic logos is a germ containing the potency of rational and spiritual evolution.

It is in the light of this potentiality that psychic history transcends the category of mechanism and becomes completely teleologic. For just as the teleologic meaning of cosmic nature is only revealed in the appearance of the psyche, so the teleology of psychic nature, and through it of all relativity, is made clear only in the ideal realization of the psychic type. This, as we have seen, is achieved by gradations in the spiritual movements of humanity and in the medium of historic individuals through whom new increments of spiritual force flow in from the transcendent logos into human channels. Thus humanity travels the toilsome road of a spiritual development through which it is enabled to approach the goal of its aspiration.

It is only from the stand-point of religion, however, that the teleology of the world can be completely understood. Religion, as we saw, is founded on a need of mediation which is inherent in the psychic nature. Even though evil had never become real the psyche is mutable and needs transcendent help to work out its spiritual destiny. Much more, then, is this assistance needful when the psyche has fallen into evil and sin has become a baleful and destructive force. The medial function must in that case also become remedial, and the psychic nature must be renovated as well as spiritualized.

But the remedial function can be no after-thought to the Absolute. For the possibility of evil in the sphere of the relative can be no after-thought. And if no after-thought, then it must be contemplated in the world-idea which underlies creation, and in which the ultimate key to the solution of the problem of evil and all other problems is to be sought. How, then, is this world-idea to be conceived? What is the highest thought of the Absolute for the relative? It must be the thought of the absolute religion. It must be a mediation that transcends ordinary historic channels although it embodies itself in the supreme historic individual. The logos of God must come down to us men from God, must enter into the sphere of relativity, into the world of the psychic logos, must achieve a consciousness of the material and corporeal, must achieve an empiric character and consciousness, and a dualistic nature in which a spiritual principle and law dominates the empirical and brings it into harmony with itself. The logos of God must enter the psychic mould and the psychic consciousness in order that it may penetrate the whole sphere of relative being with a realizing sense; in order that it may have a sense of the nature, the needs, the weaknesses, the woes, the sins, and the struggles of psychic existence. For only thus can the ideal good of the race be actualized, and only thus can the whole relative order be finally justified.

In actualizing this highest good of the relative, the logos of God becomes the ideal mediator and redeemer of an evil-smitten and struggling race. The ideal spiritual life into which man is perpetually to enter is not finite but infinite and divine. The Christ-idea is thus no product of the mythological fancy. It springs out of a necessity that is constitutional to the psychic nature. It is the spiritual ideal, which though but dimly apprehended the relative order has ever had at its heart. The Christ-idea is the true infinite ideal of humanity conceived as actualized in self-conscious and personal form. And as God is the infinite ideal of the soul conceived as actual, the Christ-idea, when it has once become a self-conscious and personal being, will embody an ideal synthesis of the human and divine.

But such an actualization cannot be the product of speculation or reflective activity. The redemption of humanity cannot be worked out in the closet of the philosopher. It must embody itself in concrete personal form in some historic individual manifestation which philosophy may reflect and translate into terms of knowledge, but which she could never create from her own resources. The logos of God thus becomes the necessary medium of the highest spiritual revelation and the highest good to humanity. It becomes the supreme revelation of the divine righteousness and truth. It embodies the divine pity, the divine love and mercy. Into it the divine helpfulness and the heart of the divine goodness enter in their fulness. It is in the vision of the logos of

God that the problem of the relative order and the world's destiny finds its most adequate solution, and it is in the light of that vision that science, philosophy, art, and religion may clasp hands in the bonds of a common faith and hope.

XVII

GOD

The greatest thought of the human spirit is the thought of God. The organ of this thought is the logos, and to attain to it the spirit must put forth its supremest effort. The genesis of the divine idea has both subjective and objective roots. Subjectively the idea of God arises as the first presupposition of the human spirit. We have seen that this is self-existence. The idea of God arises out of that of self-existence when the spirit construes it under its own highest category, namely, that of personality. The objective genesis proceeds from the idea of the world-ground. The idea of cause has coiled up in it the idea of self-activity, and when this presupposition is drawn out the idea of the world ground is born. The last step in the objective sphere is identical with that in the subjective. To the idea of a self-active world-principle the spirit applies its own highest category, and the idea of God emerges as the ground of the world.

A true insight will be able to apprehend the rationale of this process. It is the spirit's assertion of its own ideal-self; that is, of its infinite and perfect self, as actual. God is the ideal of spirit, and the idea of God is the idea of a being in whom this ideal is actual. We thus come around again to the Aristotelian conception of *purus actus*, but now translated into terms of spiritual selfhood. The idea of God is, therefore, the *ideal of the human spirit asserted as actual.* *

The problem of God's existence, or rather of his actuality, plays a great part in all human thinking. The basis of the problem is the synthesis which we have discovered in the idea of God between the concept of the ideal and the assertion of its actuality. This identifies the idea of God as it comes into the human consciousness with the spirit's assertion of its ideal and infinite self. The God-consciousness of humanity, as it may be called, is not, then, a pure intellection. It is not the absolute thought thinking itself, but it is the absolute will, in which the thought is presupposed, asserting itself. The idea of God is, therefore, the function of the logos, in which there is a synthesis of thought and will.

The various attitudes which the human spirit may take toward the problem of God's actually can be most clearly conceived from the stand-point of spirit-

---

* It is not sufficient to say that God is the ideal of the human spirit. The spirit does not leave the ideal floating about us a mere idea. But the self-assertion of its actuality is part of its essence. Spirit either affirms or denies God as an actuality. This is, I think, the real core of Des Cartes' contention that the idea of God involves the predicate of *existence*. But Des Cartes' argument is only an adumbration of the truth.

ual dialectic. We have seen how the primal intuition of being and non-being arises in the intellect and forms the basis of the self-assertion of the spirit under the category of will against non-being, in the energy of creation. This self-assertion, as we have seen, is the function of the spirit as logos. Now if we keep the dual dialectic before us we will see that the spirit may (1) deny its ideal self, and this gives rise to atheism; (2) it may assert its ideal self, which gives rise to positive theism; (3) it may assert the negative of its ideal self or the a-logos, and this will give rise to negative theism, a theory that finds the negative ground of things in God; (4) it may assert its ideal-self as the unity of being and non-being, and this will give rise to four species of pan-ontology. Of these two will be negative: (*a*) the negative pantheism of the Orient which conceives the plurality of definite existence as emanating out of a negative and indeterminate one; (*b*) naturalism which reverses the process and conceives the cosmos as emerging from a negative and indeterminate plurality. The remaining alternatives are species of positive pantheism; (*c*) a theory in which non-being is conceived simply as the self-limitation of being; this gives rise to a pantheism of the type of Spinoza in which all determination is negation; (*d*) a theory in which negation is conceived as a principle of self-diremption and non-being, therefore, as a moment of being. This gives rise to an absolutism of the type that is ordinarily ascribed to Hegel.

The insight of the dialectic will also make a very

brief criticism of these theories possible. If we penetrate to the heart of atheism we find that it involves a self-contradiction, for it is the virtual denial of self-existence, which, as we have seen, is the first presupposition of knowledge. Atheism in thus cancelling knowledge cancels itself. Negative theism arises, we saw, from the spirit's asserting its ideal as the negative of self; that is, as a spiritual being whose nature negates spiritual categories and cannot, therefore, be conceived. It is clear that this is self-contradictory, since the assertion of spiritual being carries with it the assertion of spiritual attributes. Negative theism is founded on a kind of amphiboly of the spirit in which an oscillation between positive and negative conceptions generates perpetual illusion.

In what we have called the pan-ontological theories there is a common fault that vitiates them all. In these theories the spirit asserts its ideal self as the unity of being and non-being. But this reduces difference ultimately to identity, which means stagnation and spiritual death rather than life. In asserting itself as the unity of being and non-being spirit virtually cancels itself. Now this suicidal movement may be discovered in all the theories which rest on this assumption. The Oriental thinking in its type is a species of negative pantheism, in which from a negative one the all is conceived as proceeding by emanation. But if the one negates plurality it is a contradiction to conceive a plurality as arising out of it. The world is, therefore, cancelled. Naturalism inverts the mistake by conceiving the unity of the cosmos as emerging from a negative plurality. Here, however, the negation of unity in the ground contradicts the assumption of unity in the product, and the cosmos is therefore cancelled.

The positive theories of the pantheistic type are no better off. In Spinozism difference arises through the self-limitation of being. But being can limit itself and pass into its opposite only so far as it cancels itself. Spinoza avoids this pit by asserting the unreality of being's opposite, thus cancelling difference and reducing the universe to the stillness of a moveless identity. In the second species of positive pantheism, the conception of non-being as a movement in being identifies it with being. Difference is thus cancelled and the foundation taken away from that living dialectic of spirit the affirmation of which constitutes the principal merit of Hegelism.

There remains, then, positive theism, in which the spirit asserts the ideal of its infinite and perfect self as actual. Now, if we scrutinize the logic of positive theism we will find it to be the only religious theory that keeps straight with the inner dialectic of spirit. We have seen how this dialectic starts with an intuition of being and non-being, and how this intuition rouses the will and induces the logos to go out creatively into the sphere of non-being as well as to energize internally as a principle of self-realization. This dialectic keeps wholly clear of the confusions of being and non-being, into which the theories criticised above have fallen. The logos acts on the dual intuition of identity and difference, the former being the principle of an eternal self-assertion by the divine Spirit; the latter that of an eternal opposition to non-being in the activity of creation. It is precisely this dialectical being that positive theism asserts. The God of theism is the Logos who asserts himself and creatively opposes non-being, who loves good and hates evil, who gives light and causes darkness to flee away. The God of positive theism is the God of the spirit whose vision is unclouded and whose intuitions grasp the primal dualism of reality.

The ontological proof of God's existence is, when reduced to its essence, simply the spirit's assertion of the actuality of its infinite ideal. The force of the proof lies partly in an assumption that underlies it, namely, that of self-existence. But we have seen that this assumption is the primal datum of philosophy, namely, that primal being is self-existent. Now the inner dialectic of the ontological proof is this: self-existent being is self-active, and self-activity is a spiritual category, and, therefore, the primal being is spirit. The proof asserts, if self-existence, then spiritual existence. God can be denied only by denying self-existence, which is tantamount to the spirit's denying itself, which is self-contradictory.

The founders of this proof in modern philosophy failed to clearly apprehend the inner nerve of it. Anselm defines God as a being than whom a greater cannot be conceived, and then reasons that to deny his existence would leave him less than the greatest conceivable being, which is contradictory. Had Anselm translated his quantitative conceptions into quality he would have seen the force of his reasoning to be that the last presupposition of all thinking is self-existence, and that this presupposition cannot be construed under other than spiritual categories. The primal being is, therefore, spirit. Des Cartes unfolds three aspects of the same proof: (1) That the idea of God involves the predicate of existence; (2) that the idea of God involves an adequate cause which must be an infinite and perfect being; (3) that the idea of God is the immediate presupposition of man's idea of himself, and, therefore, God exists. Underlying all these is a common dialectic process which Des Cartes did not clearly apprehend. For the aim of the ontological proof is not to establish mere existence, but rather to identify the idea of God with that of self-existence, which must be assumed. Now self-existence, as we have seen, is identical with self-activity, and self-activity is spirit. But the idea of God is that of a self-active spirit. It is therefore identical with that of the self-existent, which must be assumed. The idea of God is, therefore, the spirit's assertion of the actuality of its ideal; that is, of an infinite and perfect self.

The Kantian criticism of the ontological proof misses the fact that the relation of ideality on which the proof rests is resolvable into the self-assertion of spirit. The idea of God is identical with the idea of self-existent being, because they are both identical with that of spiritual self-activity, and spiritual self-activity is primal reality. Kant's thought had not reached the plane where such reflection is possible, and his criticism is, therefore, inconclusive.

The criticism of Kant rests, however, on the plane where doubt arises. The ontological proof contains, as we have seen, a volitional element of self-assertion, the spirit asserting its own infinite ideal as the highest actuality. Now, wherever will enters as a factor in conviction doubt is possible, for thought may abstract itself from will, and the mere abstract concept does not carry the reality of its object with it. From the stand-point of abstract thinking Kant is right and the doubt is natural.

The historical proofs from cosmology and final cause are to be regarded, primarily, as reflections entered upon by the spirit for the purpose of restoring its lost confidence in its own ideal self-assertion. The proof from cosmology is simply the reassertion in an objective form of the identity between the idea of God and that of self-existent being. Kant's criticism of this, that it is incomplete and cannot reach God without having recourse to ontology, is a piece of insight which he misuses; for, as we have seen, ontology proceeds on the same assertion of identity but finds the clinch which realizes the whole in the idea of spirit as self-activity, and, therefore, primal being. Now, cosmology falls back upon ontology to the extent of borrowing this clinch from her in order to complete its own dialectic.

What Kant should have observed is the substantial identity of the two proofs, since they involve the same dialectic in subjective and objective forms. The proof from final cause is founded on a different principle, namely, that of sufficient reason. It observes in the world-series, mainly in the sphere of living organisms, certain phenomena, manifestations of a principle of unitary individuality, which it can explain only on the supposition that there is a unitary cause, and when it further analyzes this assumption of unitary cause it finds wrapped up in it the presupposition of self-activity, which leads by a further step of reflection to the assertion of self-active spirit. The proof from final cause thus leads to the same goal that is reached by the other two proofs.

Kant's criticism of this proof is an act of logical abortion. He sees that it touches points that are common to ontology and cosmology, and assumes that it is compelled therefore to have recourse to these two arguments in order to complete its own case. What Kant fails to see is that the proof from final cause rests on a different principle from the others, that while they proceed analytically on the principle of identity, the argument from final cause proceeds synthetically on the principle of sufficient reason. It is, therefore, homogeneous, and expresses the self-assertion of spirit negatively as its refusal to be satisfied with any explanation that does not rest ultimately on a spiritual principle.

The legitimate force of these proofs in removing doubt and restoring conviction may be seen from two considerations. In the first place, they reveal the fact that whether our reflection proceeds synthetically or analytically, upon the principle of sufficient reason or upon that of identity, it reaches the same conclusion; namely, that the ultimate ground of the world must be self-existent spirit. In the second place, they fit into that dialectic which constitutes the spirit's inner activity. This dialectic, as we have seen, is dual, and includes three stages of spiritual life; first, that of thought, in which spirit thinks itself and its opposite non-being; second, that of will, in which spirit affirms itself in the principle of identity and denies its opposite in the principle of sufficient reason; third, that of love, in which spirit mediates the dual activities of identity and sufficient reason in the principle of unity. If this dialectic be conceived as the inner activity of the absolute Spirit, we arrive at the intuition of the absolute intellect as intuiting itself and its opposite; the absolute intellect and will as affirming itself and going out creatively upon its negative in the production of the creation; the absolute intellect, will, and love mediating the dual activities of the spirit and bringing the creature into unity with the Creator.

If this dialectic be conceived as the inner activity of the human spirit, the same moments will be realized as in the absolute consciousness. There must first be the self-conscious thought that thinks itself and its opposite the not-self. This supplies the inner motive to the will, and the second stage arises in which the human spirit, as thought and will, asserts itself affirmatively in the principle of identity, and negatively against its opposite in the principle of sufficient reason. But here the human spirit strikes upon the limitations of its creaturely nature. It is largely undeveloped potence passing into actuality, and its undeveloped potence limits the effective energy of will and leads to a sense of its own impotence. It also limits the spirit in this sphere qualitatively, robbing it of the creative function, for it finds that the creative intelligence has been beforehand with it, and that its function is to rethink the thoughts of the Absolute and to reproduce the creations of its power. The spirit finds that the pathway of its knowledge and experience leads it in the footsteps of a creative intelligence that has preceded it.

Now it is in this sphere where the spirit expresses itself in a synthesis of thought and will that the reflections embodied in the lines of theistic proof considered above have their rise. They arise in the human spirit's assertion of the ideal and infinite self, affirmatively and negatively, under the categories of identity and sufficient reason, as the ultimate ground of being. And they simply indicate trails which the finite intellect and will follow in their effort to make their way from the creature up to the Creator. But these proofs are not final or complete. There is a third stage in spiritual dialectic in which the spirit, as thought, will, and love asserts itself synthetically in the principle of unity. In love spirit asserts itself emotionally as well as intellectually and volitionally.

What the spirit loves as well as wills and thinks, is an object of worth or value. Modern thinking proceeding upon this recognition has shown a tendency to separate the possessions of the spirit into two groups, labelling them respectively things of knowledge and things of worth or value, the one group catering to the intellectual satisfaction of the human spirit, the other to its æsthetic and moral demands. On the basis of this distinction a further distribution of principles has been made, identity and sufficient reason being assigned to the intellect or theoretic function, while to the æsthetic is allotted the category of unity. Against this division nothing special can be urged. But the unity of the spirit is imperilled when a further step is taken and it is proposed to effect a complete divorce of the intellectual from the æsthetic and moral spheres. Motives for this divorce spring from two opposite sources: (1) from a species of neo-Kantian thought, which, having despaired of the intellect as an organ of religious truth, aims to found religion exclusively upon æsthetic and moral grounds; (2) from a rationalistic type of thinking, which resents the intrusion of æsthetic and moral considerations and aims to restrict philosophy to the plane of purely intellectual motives. It is to the interest of both these styles of thinking to separate the sphere of the æsthetic off from that of the intellect and to apply to it a different standard of valuation.

No such separation is possible. We have seen that the spirit completes itself in the third sphere of its dialectic activity in the principle of unity. But this third sphere is not purely emotional, it is the completest expression of spiritual activity, a synthesis of the intellectual, volitional, and emotional. The principle of unity is not, then, a category of emotional satisfaction simply, but it is a category that embodies the whole demand of the spirit, intellectual and volitional as well as emotional. It is the completest and most adequate form of the spirit's assertion of itself. In order, then, to complete the proof of God's existence we must supplement the lines of evidence which have been supplied by identity and sufficient reason, by the evidence of the category of unity. The very constitution of the spirit forbids that we should wrest the moral demand, as Kant does, from its affiliations with the theoretic reason, or that we should attempt, with Jacobi and Schleiermacher, to effect the same diremption between theoretic reason and feeling. The insight of the dialectic warns us that we are the rather to conceive the principles and demands of the theoretic reason as achieving their completest and ripest fruitage in the principle and demand of the moral and æsthetic nature.

The principle of unity must then be taken as having the same species of authority as the principles of identity and sufficient reason. They are all modes of spiritual self-assertion. They all embody demands of the spirit. And when the principle of unity comes with its demand for moral satisfaction in God, and for æsthetic satisfaction in a being in whom it finds the fruition of the budding hopes of its own nature, the demands cannot be dismissed as mere vain longings. They are the richest fruitage and the most adequate expression of that spiritual activity which motives the entire fabric of man's knowledge and experience.

If God *is*, how is he related to the world? This question has been virtually answered in preceding chapters. God is, in the first place, the absolute and transcendent ground of the world. The world is the product of an immanent spiritual potence which has as its immediate presupposition spiritual self-activity. This self-activity as the self-existent *prius* of all being we have found to be God. God cannot be completely immanated in the world-process. His self-activity is a presupposition of immanent potence and its denial leaves no foundation for any immanent function. God is the Creator of the world. We have already in the earlier chapters of this book endeavored to ground rationally the creative idea. It is only intelligible in the light of that living spiritual dialectic in which a key is found to so many mysteries. God as the Creator is the logos. He is God, conceived as intellect and will, asserting his divine energy in the production of the creature out of non-being. We have seen how this negative sphere arises as an intuition of the divine intellect. The logos as the divine intellect and will asserts its energy against non-being, producing out of it creature existence and the order of becoming. Thus the world-process is grounded. The immanent ground of this process is a spiritual potence which leads it in its evolution through stages of mechanism and life up to the soul of man, in which spirit becomes self-conscious.

As world-creator God is the logos, the will of the absolute spirit, uttering itself in the energy that annuls non-being and produces out of it the creature. But God is also related to the world as its builder and completer. The world as it begins is in its nature far from God; it originates as unconscious matter and mechanical force and energy. We have seen how this mechanism is rationally grounded only in a potential spiritual principle. But it is the lowest potence of spirit, unconscious, undesigning, pluralistic, and held in the clinch of necessity. The world is far from God and must be brought to him. This is the motive of the world-evolution which is a process of development along the pathway of spirit. Now God as the Creator is the logos, but God as the world-builder and developer is the unifying Spirit. The principle of his activity is unity and his motive is love. The process of evolution is not identical with creation. It presupposes and in a sense includes it just as unity includes all other principles. The process of evolution is the upward progress of the creature toward unity with the Creator. In the first stages of the world-process the motive of this unification is transcendent. The mediation which it involves is also transcendent, therefore, embodying itself in the unconscious advance of nature to higher planes of activity, the unconscious establishment of stores of potential energy as the basis of nature's advances, and the unconscious sacrifice which is involved in the achievement of higher forms of life. Though transcendent, however, the motive must be conceived as immanent in the divine activity that pulsates at the heart of the world-process. God's relation to the world can be adequately conceived only when we combine the ideas of the logos and the unifying Spirit, the one the activity that brings the world into existence out of chaos, the other the activity that moves on the face of the deep and leads the world on the pathway of order and development.

God's relations to humanity are closer because they enter more into consciousness. They are, however, generically the same as his relations to the world. God is the Creator, the Father of the human spirit. He plants in man creatively the same spiritual principle which he immanates in the world. Man is part of the world-process. But this principle in man becomes self-conscious, and thus energizes as the centre of a spiritual life that allies it to its divine author. But man is not God. He is only his image; that is, he is only a potency whose infinite and perfect actuality is God. God is, therefore, the ideal of the human spirit. And it is because the spirit is conscious of this ideal that it can call God Father. God the logos is the creative principle of humanity. We have seen how through the ideal consciousness of man an organ of close intercommunion exists between God and the human spirit, enabling God on the one hand to inform the human spirit with the norms of an ideal life, and the human spirit, on the other, to call God Father and to hold communion with him.

God as unifying Spirit is also the builder and developer of humanity. We have seen that the unifying Spirit works under the category of unity, and that its energizing motive is love. This unity is effected by mediation, and just as we saw in the world below humanity that the mediational function transcends the consciousness of the world-forces, which are its unwitting instruments in leading the world up to God, so in the evolution of humanity there is a stage where the true idea of this mediation is transcendent and its human instruments realize it unwittingly, or with only half consciousness. We have said in the chapter on Religion that the religious prophet or founder of a new dispensation must be conscious of his mission. He must intend to be God's man, speaking the thoughts and doing the will of God. But this is consistent with the existence of only a partial consciousness of the divine idea he is uttering. The prophet is only the organ which the divine energy flows into and inspires, but does not fully enlighten. Devout men of old spake as they were moved by the Holy Ghost, which had not as yet become immanent, so that it could speak in its own proper voice.

But there comes a point in the spiritual evolution of the race when God becomes immanent in the consciousness of humanity. The mode of this has been considered in the previous chapter, and the synthetic unification of the divine and human consciousness is effected in an individual soul, and the God-man is born into the world. Not only so, but the God-man consciousness is born into humanity and can no longer be foreign or merely transcendent to it. And this new birth of humanity into the divine likeness is the initiation of a new epoch in the mission of the spirit. The unifying Spirit has been in a sense a transcendent agent in human history. But now the door of a new dispensation has been opened. The logos-ideal has become a conscious possession of humanity, and through and in this logos-ideal the unifying Spirit becomes immanent in man's consciousness and functions as the regenerator, the illuminator, the sanctifier, the comforter. It performs the mediation of love more effectually than before, because now it is the spirit of the Christ, and through and in the Christ it enters the heart of humanity and leads the race on the pathway up to glory. Thus God as unifying Spirit energizing as the principle of atonement and as the heart of love, perfects the mediational work as God in the Christ reconciling the world to himself.

God is free and sovereign in his own world. It is true, as we have seen in the chapter on Non-being and Evil, that the divine option cannot include the possibility of creating an absolute and immutable world. The idea of a created Absolute, to which this is tantamount, is self-contradictory. It is true also that the relative order is one of time and development, and that not even absolute power could invert the laws of growth and development so that the spiritual should be first in the temporal order, and then the material and mechanical. For if creative power could produce at a *coup* that which is nearest to itself, then the whole labor and process of creation becomes irrational, for it would be unnecessary. Again, it is true that absolute power cannot generate a creature that shall not be mutable, and, therefore, contingent to evil. A creature that has not the contingency of evil in it must be immutable, and therefore self-existent, which is contradictory.

If absolute power be subject to these apparent limitations, how can we say that God is free and sovereign in his own world? The answer is to be found not in denying the limitations, but in showing that they are only apparent, but not real, limitations of power. In the first place, power is a function of will, and a limit arises when power falls short of will. Were the creative volition to go forth and no creation be forthcoming, or were the creature to tremble on the verge of being and then drop back into the abyss of non-being, in either case the power of the Absolute would meet a real limit and would no longer be absolute. But the very supposition that the absolute volition should contemplate the creation of another absolute outside of itself, or in addition to itself, involves, as we have seen, a monstrous self-contradiction. No real limit is involved in the avoidance of self-contradiction. There is no rationality, but the opposite, therefore, in conceiving the necessary finitude and mutability of the creature as imposing a limitation on absolute power.

But is not the subjection of the creative energy, as it enters into the world, to the orders of time and development, a limitation of the absolute power? Now, there is a sense in which this question becomes identical with the one considered above, and involves the same contradiction. It may mean why does not the absolute creative energy, if it be absolute, produce an absolute world that shall be perfect and immutable and not subject to the finite relation of time and development? We do not need to thrash over again the old irrationality.

Avoiding this absurdity the sober question is, whether the necessary subjection of relative and created being to the orders of time and development is any limitation on the power of the Absolute? To this the answer is patent. Not if time and development themselves are not conceived as absolute. The relation of the creative energy to these categories of relativity is that of their founder. They are the modes in which the energy of the Absolute enters into relative production. Development is a category, therefore, which depends on the Absolute, and instead of shutting God out of his world, or limiting his power, its whole rationality rests in its necessary presupposition of the transcendent function of the Absolute. We saw in the chapters on History and Religion, as well as in those on Cosmic, Organic, and Psychic Nature, how development necessitates the perpetual inflow of energy from absolute springs.

If development is God's creature and rests directly upon the divine energy it can contain no real limit of the divine power.

Analogous considerations bear on the problem of the temporal order. If we make time absolute, then God must work in time, and the accomplishment of his purposes will have to wait. And so between the creative fiat and the completion of the world æons must elapse sufficient to tire, if possible, even the divine patience. "God spake and it was done" thus becomes a poetic fiction, and the true idea of the deity is that of one who must wait through all the ages for the accomplishment of his purposes, while in the meantime rack and ruin are threatening the world. Such a view is irrational. Time can be conceived as only relative, and, as such, a creature of the Absolute. Lotze argues this question very subtly in his "Dictata on the Philosophy of Religion." God, he says, cannot be conceived as being *in* time. His relation to time is that of its founder. Now if God founds time, "its free ends"—this is Lotze's phrase—must converge in God. The consciousness of God will therefore be related in the same way to all the parts of time. There will be no vanishing past or oncoming future, but the whole temporal order will be what the psychologists call a "specious present." This view of time brings God into immediate relation with every part of the world. It closes up the chasm between the divine purpose and its fulfilment. It brings the world-idea in God's mind, and the world-end as it embodies itself in the far-off divine event, into immediate relation. It restores the old sublime conception of God's free sovereignty over his own world. God speaks and it is done. God does not have to wait through the long ages for the fulfilment of his designs. To God the end and the beginning are one. The weary waiting, the long ages of gradual evolution, the purpose back in eternity, and the fulfilment yonder, are ours. These things are true for us, they are necessary categories of the relative, but to God all things are present, open and immediate.

God's life is immutable and eternal. Therefore the soul's faith in God creates in it a divine thirst for immortality. The synthesis between belief in God and belief in immortality is normal and natural. Belief in God may be eclipsed, and then the rose of immortality begins to fade. But the restoration of the spirit's belief in the actuality of its own infinite ideal brings with it a revival of faith in an infinite progress of the spirit toward the ideal. The law of the soul's life, as we have seen, is that of progress toward the ideal. Whatever vivifies the ideal, therefore, and makes it real, will stimulate the ideal aspirations of the soul and gender in it the idea of a life that is commensurate with their realization. In the olden time, before the Christ-idea became a possession of humanity, when the absolute Spirit was wont to work in a transcendent manner, the idea of an immortal life could not be fully apprehended. But when the Christ-idea became immanent, then the thought of the immortal life came into the foreground, and as it grew clear and definite man's faith in it became a firm and living conviction.

There are two species of difficulty which the faith in immortality has been obliged to meet, one philosophical and the other scientific. The former takes various forms, but here, since our conception of the human soul is generically the same as Aristotle's, the difficulty will be also of the Aristotelian type. Aristotle distinguishes between the active and passive reason (νοῦς ποιητικός and νοῦς παθητικός), and connecting the latter with the corporeal principle, as a function is related to its organ, conceives that at death it perishes, and that the active reason alone is the immortal principle in the soul. Aristotle teaches the doctrine of immortality, but inasmuch as the root of personality is by him located in the passive reason, the difficulty has been to conceive the survival of any principle of personal and individual consciousness. This difficulty led the Arabian commentators on Aristotle in the middle ages, as a rule, to pronounce against the personal immortality of the soul, and this was one of the chief points of controversy between them and the later schoolmen. We avoid the difficulty, however, when we conceive the soul itself to be a developing spiritual principle which is continually passing from potence to actuality, and thus as including a synthesis of the passive and active rationality in its own constitution. This dual constitution also, as we have seen, involves the possibility of a conscious individual life distinct from that of the Absolute. It is clear that Aristotle did not realize to the full the significance of his own principle, or if so, that his commentators have not fully understood him. For if we conceive the soul as containing in its constitution the dual moments of potence and actuality, we have an idea of its nature which renders the persistence of its distinctive life both conceivable and rational.

The scientific difficulty may be stated as follows: Modern science has come to regard the brain as the organ of conscious life, and our modern thinking finds it hard to conceive any idea of conscious psychic existence apart from a brain. The difficulty seems to increase as physiological knowledge grows in accuracy and detail. Not only do we always find psychic consciousness in connection with a brain, but the method of difference seems to demonstrate that where there is no brain there can be no consciousness. A blow on the head causes a cessation of consciousness; a lesion of a particular part interrupts the flow of some portion of the conscious stream. Brain conditions seem to determine conscious states, and as an organized whole as well as in its molecular constitution nerve-tissue seems to constitute an indispensable condition of psychic life.

This difficulty would be insurmountable, we think, if the relation between the human soul and its corporeal organism were conceived as one of mutually exclusive entities. The fact that it is ordinarily so conceived simply testifies to the survival of the Cartesian dualism. The whole theory of this treatise is, however, a denial of that view and an assertion of a merely relative distinction between them, one that is mediated by a spiritual principle. Matter is the first potency of spirit, and mechanism and its laws are spiritual in their foundations. Now as the soul is not only a part of the world-energy, but also an epitome and synthesis of it, there is logically involved in the idea of the soul that of a principle which holds in it a duality of potencies, material and spiritual. We thus transfer the bond which binds the material and spiritual together from an external position to its seat in the soul itself. And by so doing we arrive at the conception of a dual psychic constitution, which contains in itself the germs of both material and spiritual organization. The corporeal organism may dissolve, then, and the basal constitution of the soul will still remain intact as the norm of a continuous life of conscious growth and activity. And when the idea of an ultimate Psychic constitution has once been achieved, the presumption of science changes, for it is then seen that the dissolution of the body does not necessitate the destruction of the soul.

Thus the negative presumptions of philosophy and science are overcome, and the spirit is left free to assert its own ideal life. It is the same voice of the spirit under the same category of unity that demands both the divine ideal and the unending life. It is in this dual synthesis of God and immortality that the soul finds the satisfaction of its thirst for unity and completeness. In the same synthesis is found an unfailing well-spring of joyous and hopeful activity both for the individual soul and for humanity.

Man is born an heir to immortal existence. The voice that cries out in him for an unending life is the utterance of his deepest nature. But the soul tragedy of modern life is that the intellect has grown sceptical and contradicts the deeper voice of the spirit. The spirit cries out for immortality, but the intellect says, Cease your striving, nor vainly imagine that the universe exists only for your delectation. But the soul's demand is vital and its disappointment means death. So the waters of existence become bitter to the palate, and the fine spiritual nature, robbed of its holiest birthright, plunges into pessimistic despair and longs for some Lethe stream in which to forget its troubled dream. Or, if it wills to live bravely on and work, the joys of life become apples of Sodom in its mouth and the solid structure of the world that surrounds it shrinks into a mere veil of illusion behind which stalks, not Nirvana, but the gaunt spectre of Abaddon. For when the immortal hope is gone, life shrinks into a thing of shreds and patches and all philosophy becomes in truth "a meditation on death and annihilation."

XVIII

SPIRITUAL ACTIVITY

We have seen that primal being can be conceived only as self-activity. Self-activity is activity that contains its primal impulse within itself. Self-activity is also self-conscious activity. And we have seen that self-conscious activity is self-asserting and self-realizing. We mean this when we say that primal being is spirit.

The dialectic of spirit is the form of its activity. The dialectic presupposes the primal motive. Why being should be active is a question that transcends all answer. We assume it when we say primal being is self-activity. Its first impulse to action is identical with itself. Now this first impulse is the initial step of the dialectic. The moments of it are all pulsations of self-assertion. The initial pulsation, as we have seen, is one of intellection. Being is primally intelligent and rational. Its first activity is thought, a thought in which the primal impulse embodies itself. It thinks itself. But the primal impulse reveals the primal distinction. The thought that thinks itself also thinks its opposite. It is as impossible to derive difference as it is to derive identity. They are involved in the primal impulse of being. It is the essence of spirit to think the same and the different.

The result of the primal impulse is the dual intuition of being's self, and being's not-self, or of being and non-being. It is here that we strike upon the crucial point of the whole dialectic of spirit. When in this primal activity being thinks the not-self, does it simply negate itself and then by another act negate the negation, and thus reach self-affirmation through negation? Or, putting it in another form, is it being that goes out as the nothing and then returns again as a higher form of being? This is the ordinary Hegelian interpretation. We think a radical reform is needed at this cardinal point. Being never denies itself except in a relative sense. Its negation is directed against its opposite. We would then construe the movement of the primal impulse as follows. When in accordance with the original dual category being thinks the not-self, it thinks objectively, and its intuition is of that which negates self; that is, the opposite of self. Now the intuition of that which is opposite to self is a point of reaction for what is called the return upon self, which means the reassertion of the self against its opposite, or the reassertion of identity against difference. We may speak by a species of dialectic license of this movement as a return of being out of nothing upon itself, or as a return of identity out of difference, if we avoid the contradictory assumption that being has ever lost itself in nothing, or identity in difference. The distinction here is just as primal as the thinking itself, for it is constitutional to it. The primal movement of spirit, as we have said, is self-assertion, and in this primal intellection it is self-assertion through identity and difference. This does not mean, however, that spirit thinks itself as the same and then thinks itself as the different; that is, as the not-self. Spirit is not the arch-juggler of the universe. What is meant is something simpler. Spirit thinks itself as the same; that is, the self becomes conscious of itself. Spirit thinks the not-self as different; that is, the self becomes conscious of a not-self, as its different or opposite. The primal dialectic of thinking is between the same and the different. But they are never identified. The intellectual impulse has nothing erudite about it. To it being and nothing are not identical but opposite, and the true genius of intellection is sacrificed whenever this distinction is obscured.

To be clear on this cardinal point settles the whole dialectic of spirit. The other moments follow from the nature of spirit as self-conscious activity. The intuition of the negative or non-being constitutes a motive that determines the procession of the spirit. The primal impulse to self-assertion in view of this intuition becomes self-assertion against the negative, in a volitional form; that is, as the will to suppress and annul the negative. Now, absolute will is self-active and moves upon the negative or non-being as energy of creation. The creative impulse is not primal, if we use the term in a logical sense, but has as its presupposition the activity of absolute intellection which reveals the negative sphere. Creation is thus both rational and volitional and may be conceived as the will to annul non-being by the production of forms of being. But here again our thinking must avoid entanglement. In creation the distinction of being and non-being is not annulled. Creation is not a procession of the Absolute in a relative and finite dress. Relativity and finitude are more than appearances; they are constitutional to the creature. The absolute will does not finitate or limit itself in the creation. The idea of absolute self-limitation involves that of the annihilation of energy and is self-contradictory.

The only possible concept of a creature is that of a nature that contains opposite momenta of being and non-being. Plato in the Timæus clothes a true intuition in symbols. The Demiurge compounds opposite ingredients, the same and the other, into a third existence, in which the intractable nature of the other is compressed into synthesis with the same. The creative energy annuls non-being by generating a created nature into which non-being, while it enters as a dividual, separative, dissolutive condition, is held in subordination by the unitary principle of being; that is, the principle of self-conscious spiritual activity.

The dual nature of the creature thus originates, a nature that is ever in a state of flux, as Plato says, and that is ever oscillating between the opposite poles of being and non-being. And it is this dual nature of the creature, as we saw in the first chapters of this book, that renders it open to change and evolution. Being does not limit itself in the creation, but the negative element is the limit that reduces spiritual energy to potence and thus makes development essential.

Now, it is in connection with the evolution of the creature that the third movement in the dialectic of spirit arises. Evolution is to be conceived as the gradual development of the principle of being in the nature of the creature, from potence to actuality, through a progressive suppression or transcendence of the negative. Being can grow only through the transcendence, the annulling of non-being. And non-being can be completely transcended only in the unification of the creature with the Creator through an infinite approximation. Spirit's primal impulse of self-assertion, in view of the negative character of the creature, its distance and alienation from actualized spirit, is to go out in the energy of love as a developing and mediating force of unification. But here again our thinking must keep clear of entanglements. It is not the unity of being and non-being that is conserved in this developing process. Non-being is annulled and suppressed from the beginning to the end of it. It is the unity of being and becoming, the creature and the Creator, that is conserved. And the negative side of this conserving process is the war against and the suppression of non-being.

This dialectic of spirit which thus passes through the moments of negation, creation and unification is completely realized only when we conceive it in a twofold manner, (1) on its subjective side as a logical self-completion of spirit in the unity of thought, volition, and love; (2) on its objective side as the progressive completion of the creature through the momenta of creation and evolution, culminating in the final mediation and unity of creature and Creator.

Thus we conceive the movement of absolute spirit under its own categories. Subject to the limitations of its finite nature the dialectic of the human spirit is to be conceived under the same categories. We have already in the chapter on Knowledge developed the process of the intellectual life in which it travels through the categories of identity and difference and sufficient reason up to that of unity, under which it realizes the rational ideal of knowledge. We have only to translate the stages of this progress into volitional terms in order to see how the whole practical life of man becomes a battle with the negative, a struggle to overcome the world. The life of the spirit is a conflict waged positively, as the spirit's assertion of itself in the progress of its own inner evolution and the development of its spiritual potences, negatively as a battle against negation and evil, and as a refusal to be satisfied with anything short of the highest good.

And this ideal is realized only through the unifying activity of love. In the absolute sphere unity of the Creator and his world is effected, as we have seen, only through the activity of love manifesting itself on the broad arena of nature and humanity and realizing itself through mediation and sacrifice. This is also the law of the human spirit. In the unifying activity of love the spirit asserts itself negatively in the progressive annulment of the negative forces that hinder spiritual development; in its progressive triumph over sin and evil in the individual and common life of humanity; in the war of extermination that it perpetually wages against selfishness and falsehood. It asserts itself positively in the rise of the spirit's activity, through comprehension, into ever larger and larger spheres of life. Thus, for example, the life of the individual is transcended and comprehended in the larger life of the family. That of the family is transcended and comprehended in the larger life of the community and the institutions of church and state, while the supreme unification is reached in the sphere of religion where the larger life of humanity is brought into ideal harmony with God.

Thus the larger life of the human spirit realizes itself, but not without renunciation. The suppression of the negative is an inseparable accompaniment of positive growth. The spirit, in order to enter into the higher and broader life, must deny its lower and less developed self by throwing off restrictions and hinderances. In order to enter into the larger life of the family, the state, the church, or the race, the old man must be put off and the new man must be put on. And that largest and supremest life of the spirit, which it enters into in the religious sphere, the life with God, is conditioned on the supremest act of self-renunciation. Here the war with the negative reaches its final stage, where on the one side the demand for self-renunciation and annulment is most absolute, while on the other the comprehension and unification is most complete. For through all its renunciations the spirit carries its true self with it; only the negative, the imperfect, the evil is progressively cast aside, while the real self ever increases its riches as it merges into larger and more comprehensive spheres of activity.

We have only to complete this idea of the struggle of the human spirit with the idea of its dependence upon its absolute ground, in order to obtain a key to the whole life of humanity. The human spirit cannot conserve its own development, but in unity with the absolute source of its being it may, through constant accessions of transcendent strength and grace, be able to overcome all the forces of negation and evil and to advance continually in the progressive stages of an endless life.

CONCLUSION

Looking back over the path we have travelled in this inquiry several reflections suggest themselves in conclusion. In the first place, we have found in personality the highest category of interpretation in the spheres of both the relative and the Absolute. Now personality is first known as a psychological fact in the soul's experience, and the inference would seem to follow that all philosophy rests on psychology. This we shall not attempt to deny. The spirit of the knower must be able to find in itself the clews to all the mysteries of being, so far as they may be resolved. At the same time the dependence of philosophy on psychology cannot be construed in any narrow or exclusive sense. Philosophy is not simply an extension of psychology. An inquiry such as the present one has been, is fitted to open our eyes to the fact that our psychological categories only become philosophically competent after they have, so to speak, passed through the historic medium and embodied themselves objectively in the experience of humanity. The psychological categories must, in short, be translated from subjective to objective universals. The fact that only history is competent to this translation renders that insight which only comes from a real knowledge of the historic evolution of thought indispensable to philosophy. The true organ of philosophy is constituted by a synthesis of the spiritual insights of both psychology and history.

The truth of this is demonstrated in the instance of personality. The riches of this category never would yield themselves to introspective and subjective analysis alone. Far less would they give up their secrets to the exclusive analysis of the individual consciousness. The full significance of personality emerges only in the objective thinking and the spiritual experience of the race, and it is only when the spirit finds its subjective categories embodied for it in these objective forms that they become adequate to the demands of philosophy.

There may be some who will think that in the attempt to break the agnostic limitations we have gone too far toward the gnostic extreme. But such persons may be reassured. The intelligence of the creature will always find that the Creator has been beforehand with it, so that, penetrate as far as it may, it will find itself only tracing the footsteps of an absolute intelligence that has preceded it. Besides, the aim of this whole inquiry has been to penetrate the mysteries of the Absolute only so far as may be necessary in order to discover how it rationally grounds the relative order. The category of personality conceived as an immanent activity of being gives us this insight, but we know not, and doubtless can never know, what abysses of the Absolute still remain unpenetrated. The category of personality does not abolish mystery, but simply lifts the veil a little way and reveals a glimpse of the creative energy in its relation to the world.

Our inquiry has also tested the value of the dual categories being and non-being in solving philosophic problems and in developing the outlines of a coherent and comprehensive theory. Whatever speculative difficulties may yet remain, the working power of these conceptions can no longer be questioned. It may be maintained with Hegel that the highest category is an absolute idea which comprehends the dual moments, being and non-being, within itself. To this we may yield a qualified assent, provided this idea be translated into spirit and its dialectic be conceived as on its affirmative side, self-affirmation, but on its negative side the denial of its opposite. The reform in Hegelism, which has been urged throughout this inquiry, may be expressed in the following statement: being must be identified with spirit. The inner movement of spirit is a dual dialectic in which spirit asserts itself and denies its opposite. The dual movement is thus immanent in being. But the negative which spirit denies is not in being. It is an oppositive excluded conception, which spirit forever wars against and suppresses, but which never passes into its opposite. The negative activity of spirit thus becomes from one point of view an outgoing oppositive energy, as distinguished from the immanent activity of self-affirmation, while from another point of view it is the volitional energy of creation and development. This conception of absolute spirit in its dual activity renders its whole relation to the relative order, including evil and negation, both intelligible and rational.

The current thinking of our time can find no better answer to the question how it happens that an absolute energy produces only a relative and imperfect creature, than the assertion that the Absolute imposes a limit upon itself and voluntarily restrains its creative energies within finite bounds when otherwise the result would have been infinite and perfect. Now it is clear that no theory of arbitrary self-restraint can supply the ground of a rational explanation, and if the conception is to be saved from becoming positively irreligious it must be subsumed under the category of the good. The only motive, in other words, that can make such self-restraint reasonable must be derived from the absolute goodness. But in view of the actual evil that has arisen out of the finitude and imperfection of things the goodness of the Absolute cannot be vindicated, if, as the theory in question implies, the creative will had before it an option between the generation of an infinite and perfect world, and one that is finite and imperfect. For the fact remains, on this supposition, that a world-scheme which involves the contingency and actuality of evil has been preferred to one from which these features are absent.

A rational insight into the negative cuts the knot of the difficulty by helping us to see that the supposition of such an option is irrational and that the only option conceivably before the absolute will is a choice between pure negation and a finite and relative order of being. It is no impeachment of absolute power that its outgoing energy does not generate another absolute alongside of itself, nor is it any impeachment of the absolute goodness that it prefers to non-being a relative and finite order of being which involves the contingency of evil. We have seen that the true significance of the world-order can be seen only in the light of the highest conceptions of religion, and that from the stand-point of religion evil becomes a subordinate though real feature of the world, while the good stands supreme as the end and rationale of its whole history and development.

Furthermore, our reflection enables us to conceive a rational solution of the issues between monism and dualism, on the one hand, and idealism and realism on the other. A monistic theory of reality which identifies it with being must always be inadequate since the real must include the opposite of being, which can never be identified with being without transgressing basal principles. Also any monistic theory must be inadequate which ignores the distinction between the Absolute and the relative and seeks to apply a unitary principle, let it be spiritual or material, without regard to that distinction. For in that case, if we start from absolute being, we will miss the actual duality of the relative, whereas if we take our departure from the relative we will never be able to conceive any point where a transition of the real from relative to absolute is possible. And this inability will carry with it the impossibility of assurance as to the existence of the Absolute.

A rational metaphysic will admit the distinction between being and reality, and while asserting the unitary character of the one will acknowledge the duality of the other. The real includes the negative of being. It will also admit the distinction between being and becoming, and while asserting the unitary character of being will admit the duality of becoming. In short, a rational metaphysic is identical with a spiritualistic theory of reality, which, postulating an absolute spirit as the self-existent principle of things, is able to see not only how the necessity of non-being springs from this postulate, but also how the negative supplies a necessary datum of the relative, accounting for its modified and dualistic character. Monism is right when it says there is only one principle of being, but it is mistaken when it identifies being and reality, and on that basis denies the reality of the negative.

The issue between idealism and realism is not so stringent. There are several types of theory which a spiritualistic metaphysic will reject. One of these is a type of ontologic idealism which suppresses volition and feeling in the interests of abstract thought. Another is a species of subjective psychological idealism which ignores the ontologic aspect of reality and completely identifies the object of knowledge with the subjective psychic process through which it is apprehended. Still a third type is a species of realism which assumes the distinction between spirit and matter to be absolute, thus, by implication at least, carrying the duality of substances up into the nature of the Absolute.

The truth which metaphysics is chiefly concerned to assert is that the real is primally spiritual. A spiritualistic theory leads, as we have seen, to the recognition of a distinction between the Absolute and the relative and the inclusion of both in the synthesis of reality. This makes it impossible to reduce the relative to mere appearance. The relative is real. It has its roots in the Absolute, but it is not a mere *schein* of the Absolute. We have seen that relativity has a distinctive constitution and type which make it analogous to a word that, once uttered, cannot be recalled. The word of the Absolute endureth forever. Moreover, in the relative sphere the material is not a mere *schein* of the spiritual. We have seen that the law of relativity is, first the material, then the spiritual; that the spiritual categories are the highest. But this does not mean the suppression of the material or its reduction to unreality. In achieving the spiritual, the material and mechanical are gone through but not left behind. The material stands there hard and durable, and the moment of mechanism is ever present in the highest manifestations of spirit. The world is a solid and firm-jointed reality which confronts the knower and fills his categories with objective content from the beginning to the end of the process of experience.* A theory which thus asserts a system of reality at the heart of which pulsates the personal energy of spirit may be idealistic in its conception of the *mode* of knowledge, since knowledge and reality must be distinguished, but it will be realistic in its metaphysic. Not the idea, but concrete spirit is the primal unit of being. If, however, the idea should be identified with concrete spirit and enriched with a content of volition and love, and then its exponent should cling to idealism as the best designation of his creed, the issue is not one over which philosophy need go to pieces.

Again, in view of conclusions already established, we think a settlement of the issue between naturalism and supernaturalism becomes practicable. Huxley points with some concern to the victorious march of naturalism in our modern thinking. Everywhere the supernatural is falling into discredit, and even religion, if it would avoid the charge of superstition, must assume a naturalistic garb. Now there is a scientific naturalism which is sound and, in fact, necessary. Science deals with causation and development, and we have seen that these are categories of the natural series. Not only the sciences of nature but psychology and history are obliged to be naturalistic in this sense. Now between such naturalism and spiritualism there is no issue. The cause and the movement may be both spiritual and material. When, however, naturalism is carried over

* In this we simply reassert the position which McCosh and the Scottish thinkers maintain against what may be called phenomenal idealism.

into metaphysics as an exclusive category it becomes false. The first presupposition of metaphysics is the Absolute, which is both transcendent and supernatural. The metaphysical ground of an adequate world-theory is a synthesis of the natural and phenomenal with this supernatural ground. Metaphysics must affirm a synthesis of natural and supernatural, and this synthesis must also be found at the heart of every adequate philosophy of religion. The suppression of the supernatural carries with it the death of true naturalism.

Lastly, we have in our inquiry been led to see how a rational solution of the modern antinomy between the ideas of immanence and transcendence is possible. We do not any longer need to work the old treadmill of annulling one in the supposed interest of the other, for we have seen that they are not contradictory, but rather complementary conceptions. The first presupposition of all being is a self-existent Absolute which stands as the transcendent ground and principle of the world. The world is generated by the outgoing volitional energy of this Absolute. But the creative energy itself enters into the world as the immanent spring of its existence and development. The Creator is in his world, but he is not wholly swallowed up by it. A synthesis of immanence and transcendence is necessary in order to rationalize the world. We are not obliged, then, to be either deists or pantheists, but true philosophic insight will lead us to a religious position in which the shortcomings of both are escaped.

www.ingramcontent.com/pod-product-compliance
Lightning Source LLC
Chambersburg PA
CBHW030808230426
43667CB00008B/1112